THE COMPLETE MARTIAL ARTS TRAINING MANUAL

AN INTEGRATED APPROACH

ASHLEY P. MARTIN

TUTTLE PUBLISHING
Tokyo • Rutland, Vermont • Singapore

Acknowledgements

I would like to thank the following people
for their help in creating this book:

Nita Martin—for extensive help researching and editing
James Bailey and Carlos Martos—for taking part in the photo shoot
Andrew Kuc—for taking part in shooting the DVD

— Ashley P. Martin

Published by Tuttle Publishing, an imprint of Periplus Editions (HK) Ltd., with editorial offices at 364 Innovation Drive, North Clarendon, Vermont 05759 U.S.A. and at 61 Tai Seng Avenue #02-12, Singapore 534167.

Library of Congress Cataloging-in-Publication Data

Martin, Ashley, 1972-
The complete martial arts training manual : an integrated approach / Ashley P. Martin.
    p. cm.
Includes bibliographical references.
ISBN 978-0-8048-4086-6 (pbk.)
1. Martial arts--Handbooks, manuals, etc. I. Title.
GV1101.M37 2010
796.815--dc22
2009033441

ISBN: 978-0-8048-4086-6

Important notice: Whilst every effort has been made to ensure that the content of this book is as safe and technically accurate as possible, neither the author nor the publishers can accept responsibility for any injury or loss sustained as a result of the use of this material. It is the responsibility of the individual to ensure that they are fit to participate and they should seek medical advice from a qualified professional where appropriate.

Distributed by

North America, Latin America & Europe
Tuttle Publishing
364 Innovation Drive
North Clarendon, VT 05759-9436 U.S.A.
Tel: 1 (802) 773-8930
Fax: 1 (802) 773-6993
info@tuttlepublishing.com
www.tuttlepublishing.com

Japan
Tuttle Publishing
Yaekari Building, 3rd Floor
5-4-12 Osaki
Shinagawa-ku
Tokyo 141 0032
Tel: (81) 3 5437-0171
Fax: (81) 3 5437-0755
tuttle-sales@gol.com

Asia Pacific
Berkeley Books Pte. Ltd.
61 Tai Seng Avenue #02-12
Singapore 534167
Tel: (65) 6280-1330
Fax: (65) 6280-6290
inquiries@periplus.com.sg
www.periplus.com

14 13 12 11 10   6 5 4 3 2 1

Printed in Singapore

TUTTLE PUBLISHING® is a registered trademark of Tuttle Publishing, a division of Periplus Editions (HK) Ltd.

CONTENTS

INTRODUCTION

Learning the Aspects of Fighting

There are many aspects of fighting. A combatant might try to strike his opponent using punches and kicks in an effort to either incapacitate him, perhaps with a knockout blow, or to weaken him so that it would be subsequently easier to land that finishing blow. This immediately leads to another aspect of combat, that is to defend against such attacks, either by blocking them with a tough part of the body, such as an arm or a knee, or to deflect them with a well-timed parry, or to avoid the attack altogether with skillful evasion. Very often in a fight, combatants will find themselves at such a close range that punches and kicks become impossible to use effectively. In close range fighting, elbows and knees might fly while the fighters grapple–pushing and pulling each other in an attempt to gain an advantage. The grappling might allow one fighter to trip or throw the other to the ground. The fight might end there, especially if the ground is hard and the fallen warrior lands heavily. Very often the fight will continue on the ground where a skilled martial artist will look for ways to painfully force joints against their natural range of motion, or to apply a strangle hold that will render an opponent unconscious.

There are many martial arts, all differing in their approach to fighting, but there are few that deal with all the many aspects of fighting. Instead it is more common for a particular martial art to consider a few aspects more important and to focus on them. In order to truly understand the martial arts and be able to confidently defend yourself, you need to cover all the aspects of fighting. One way to do this is to train in more than one martial art and so picking up complementary skills that fill the gaps that one lone martial art would otherwise leave.

If you have already studied a martial art, this book offers guidance on how to expand your skill set and become a complete martial artist, filling the gaps in your knowledge. If you are completely new to the world of martial arts you might be wondering which of the many martial arts to learn. This book covers the range of martial arts popular today, allowing you to find the one that fits your needs and interests.

CHAPTER ONE—**THE WAY OF THE WARRIOR**

Martial arts have played various roles throughout history. They have evolved from being necessary tools used for fighting wars into methods of civil self-defense and self-cultivation or into sporting activities. Chapter 2 examines the advantages and disadvantages of competitive sparring. It also discusses the limitations of studying a single martial art in isolation and the importance of cross training in different martial arts.

CHAPTER TWO—**A CATALOG OF MARTIAL ARTS**

There are dozens of martial arts–hundreds or even thousands if all the different styles and sub-styles are counted. Chapter 3 gives a panoramic view of the different martial arts that are currently popular and analyzes how they came into being, how they are related, and what they have to offer to someone practicing them.

CHAPTER THREE—**COMBAT BASICS**

Before looking at the specific techniques that make up martial arts, it is important to examine the basic elements that make up a fight. Broadly speaking, there are three phases: the striking phase, the grappling phase, and the ground-fighting phase. Chapter 4 discusses these phases of combat and how they relate to each other. The basic fighting positions from which techniques are performed are also described in this chapter

CHAPTER FOUR—**HAND AND ELBOW STRIKES**

The advantage of using your fists and elbows to strike is that they are fast and relatively easy to learn as they don't require any special flexibility training. Chapter 5 describes how to make a fist so that you can correctly punch as well as how to use the basic punches. It also covers how you can fight at close range using elbow strikes and how to use the slightly more exotic open-handed strikes.

CHAPTER FIVE—**DEFENSES**

Being able to defend yourself against an incoming attack is at the heart of self-defense. Chapter 6 describes how attacks can be blocked or parried using your arms. It also covers how to defend using evasive techniques like slipping or ducking which leave your hands free to counter attack.

CHAPTER SIX—**FOOT AND KNEE STRIKES**

The most impressive moves in the martial arts are kicks. Chapter 7 describes how to perform these powerful attacks as well as how to use knee strikes when at close range.

CHAPTER SEVEN—**BREAK FALLING**

Before practicing takedowns you need to learn how to fall safely. Chapter 8 describes the various ways of safely landing after you have been thrown or tripped. It also describes ways of recovering after the fall so that you can return to a fighting position.

CHAPTER EIGHT—**TAKEDOWNS**

Takedowns are techniques that bring your opponent from a standing position down onto the ground. This can be a damaging action itself or it can be a way to progress to ground fighting. Chapter 9 describes the various ways that you can take an opponent down to the ground using throws that lift and then drop an opponent, reaps that take an opponent's legs away from under him, and sacrifice throws that drag an opponent down to the ground.

CHAPTER NINE—**LOCKS AND HOLDS**

Locks and hold are techniques that can be used in close range grappling either on the ground or while standing. They can be used to restrain an opponent or to force them to submit. Chapter 10 describes how to use some of the more common arm bars that lock the elbow, wrist locks that twist or hyperextend the wrist, and chokeholds that can be used to restrict air or blood flow.

CHAPTER TEN—**GROUND FIGHTING**

Once a fight goes to the ground, high kicks and fancy footwork become useless. Fighting on the ground is not just about brute strength, however, and Chapter 11 describes some of the ways that you can gain the advantage while on the ground. This includes ways of pinning your opponent, the various guards that can be used to defend yourself, ways of getting past an opponent's guard, and how to use strikes while on the ground.

CHAPTER ELEVEN—
STRETCHING FOR THE MARTIAL ARTIST

Flexibility is essential for a martial artist especially if you want to do high kicks. Flexible joints are also useful if you are going to take part in any grappling because a greater range of movement will give you the edge when trying to escape or reach for a hold. Chapter 12 describes various ways of improving the flexibility of your legs (both to the front and to the side), your arms, and your back.

CHAPTER TWELVE—
NUTRITION FOR THE MARTIAL ARTIST

Nutrition is an often-overlooked element that contributes to fitness. This aspect is particularly important for the martial artist who wishes to compete in tournaments where being able to make a specific weight category while maximizing performance can be a factor. Chapter 13 explains how the body uses food, how to gain muscle mass, how to lose fat, and important concepts for martial artists such as glycemic index which can affect energy reserves while competing or training.

It is wonderful. It truly is. It is the only thing that is real!
It's you against me, it's challenging another guy's manhood.
With gloves. Words cannot describe that feeling—of being a man,
of being a gladiator, of being a warrior. It's irreplaceable.

~ Sugar Ray Leonard

CHAPTER ONE

The Way of the Warrior

The most common perception of a martial art is that of an oriental fighting system: throwing punches and flying kicks. Of course, systems of fighting are not restricted to the East. Boxing, wrestling, and fencing are just some of the martial arts that are common in Europe.

Martial arts can be broadly categorized into three main types: striking, grappling, and weapons arts. This simple classification makes it easier to get a handle on the diverse range of martial arts that exist. Although the original objective of the martial arts was to train individuals how to fight, this is no longer the only reason that people take up training. There are many other benefits to such training. For example, you may just be interested in finding out about exotic training traditions and history, you may be attracted to the health and fitness benefits, or you may indeed be looking to become a competitor.

Some find an alternative categorization system useful in tackling this subject. Internal and external, similar to soft and hard, classes can be used give a different kind of sense about the system. This is primarily a philosophical classification that comes from traditional Chinese martial arts, with an external system being outwardly physical in its nature with big blocks and attacks; and an internal system taking a more subtle approach through fluid movements.

Inevitably, most martial arts contain some sort of sparring. The original aim of sparring practice was to help to train people to fight. However, the false nature of set piece sparring, and sparring with restrictions in competitions can give you a false sense of your ability to defend yourself in a real life situations where there are no rules. That is not to say that sparring doesn't have an important place in any training system. Indeed, taking part in competitive sparring is always overall more realistic than any training method that uses a collaborating partner, no matter how well intentioned the methodology.

Focusing on a single martial art is certainly the way to start your training. However, if your objective is to be a well-rounded fighter, then looking at what the other martial arts have to offer will form an important part of your training. This has led to the emergence of mixed martial arts (MMA) where techniques from many martial arts can be used. This type of training has led to well-rounded, more complete martial artists.

What is a Martial Art?

A martial art is a codified system of fighting. Many martial arts teach you how to fight with a weapon, others are concerned with unarmed fighting. Some martial arts are intended for use against multiple assailants, while others have been designed to duel against a single skilled opponent. Martial arts have one object in common—to gain an advantage in combat through the development of superior fighting skill.

Many people think of martial arts as being primarily a phenomenon unique to the Far East but, in fact, every culture has its own inherited martial tradition. The ancient Greek Olympic games (776 BC-393 AD) included boxing and wrestling events. From 648 BC, they also included an event that was called *pankration*, which literally means "all powers," reflecting the fact that competitors could use almost any attack that they wanted. The only techniques that were not allowed were eye gouges and bites, so competitors would use a combination of boxing and wrestling moves in addition to kicking techniques.

Historically, martial training was focused on weapon based martial arts because of their use on the battlefield. For example, in Japan, the samurai would fight primarily with the long sword, using kenjutsu, but for those times when they could not use a sword, they had an unarmed fighting art called jujutsu. Similarly, in Europe, many fencing books were produced between the 15th and 17th century. The long sword was held in the highest regard but a number of combat forms were taught alongside swordsmanship including stick fighting, armored combat, mounted combat, and unarmed grappling, as well as the use of various weapons, such as daggers and pole arms.

It was only after the Renaissance that martial arts in Europe started to divide into different fields: civilian dueling (self-defense), most commonly with the rapier; sporting activity such as boxing, wrestling, or stick fighting; and military training which evolved with the military thinking of the time—during the 19th century this would have consisted of bayonet, saber, and the lance.

By the 20th century, martial arts had begun to be taught in schools and universities. In Japan, judo and karate found their way into the public school system and it was in the Universities of Tokyo that these martial arts evolved into sporting activities. In the West, boxing and wrestling became increasingly accepted as sports. For example, the Universities of Oxford and Cambridge have had an official annual boxing match since 1896 and, in the United States, boxing was introduced in the 1920s both for its recreational value and for physical conditioning, leading to intercollegiate boxing leagues. Wrestling has been an intercollegiate sport in the United States since 1900 and this soon spread to wrestling tournaments for high school students.

Following the Second World War, there was an increase in exposure in the West to the Eastern fighting arts. Some martial arts masters from the East emigrated to the West to set up schools open to the paying public. Following a kung fu craze in the 1970s, brought about by Hong Kong "chop socky" movies, there was a rapid rise in popularity of Eastern martial arts, especially karate, judo, kung fu, aikido, and jujutsu.

Categories of Martial Arts

From the strong linear attacks of karate to the fast, light movements of Wing Chun or the big throws of judo, the world of martial arts is wide and diverse. Each martial art has its own traditions and each emphasizes different aspects of how to fight. It is possible to break down the different martial arts into three categories based on their emphasis.

The striking arts focus on attacking by striking with various parts of the body, typically punching with the fist or kicking with the feet. Practitioners of these arts will usually also focus on how to defend against kicking and punching attacks, either through deflecting these attacks, by evading them, or by simply blocking them with a forearm or a shin.

The grappling arts focus on close quarters fighting involving throwing their opponent or applying locks or holds to restrain them. Training in the grappling arts also includes ways to escape from locks and holds and ways to counter attempts to grab or throw.

The weapon arts focus on how to fight using weapons. Individual arts will usually focus on a single type of weapon or on a small set of weapons. They will usually practice ways to defend against someone who is also using that particular weapon.

A CATEGORIZATION OF MARTIAL ARTS BASED ON THEIR EMPHASIS	
Examples of striking arts	Karate, Taekwondo, Capoeira, Savate, Boxing, Muay Thai, Kung Fu
Examples of grappling arts	Judo, Jujutsu, Aikido, Wrestling
Examples of weapon arts	Kendo, Iaido, Fencing, Eskrima

In many cases, a martial art will fit neatly into one of these categories. If someone practices kendo, then they are going to learn how to fight with a sword, Japanese style. If they want to learn how to fight if they lose their weapon, then they would be studying jujutsu, which pretty much evolved just to fill this gap.

Just because a martial art focuses on a certain aspect of fighting does not mean that it necessarily excludes other ways of fighting. For example, jujutsu, despite being mainly concerned with throwing an opponent or applying locks, does include the art of striking and the art of blocking. It also includes methods for defending against various weapons. Conversely, karate practitioners will spend almost all their time either practicing kicks, punches, and other strikes or defending against those strikes. However, the karate forms (kata) are composed of a significant number of moves that are essentially close range grappling techniques. Many karate practitioners do not fully appreciate this and begrudgingly learn kata so that they can pass their next grading examination. However, the great karate masters of the past seem quite clear on this point: the kata are the most important part of karate.

So, in many cases, the category that a martial art can be placed in is a bit of a gray area. It's not as if the martial art excludes certain techniques, but more that the practitioners prefer to focus on a specific aspect. So why do so many martial artists diligently practice some elements of combat skill while neglecting others that are essential in many combat situations?

SPECIALIZATION IS GOOD

Specializing in one aspect of fighting is better than learning all the aspects badly. Learning a martial art is difficult and it can take many years to master even one aspect of fighting.

MARTIAL ARTS AS SPORT

Many people train in a martial art to compete, not to fight. This distinction might seem a bit subtle when watching boxers doing their best to score a knockout blow or a judoka applying a chokehold. The important difference is that there are rules. The boxer cannot kick his opponent (or bite his ear as seems to happen from time to time) without disqualification. Neither can the judo man, nor can he even throw a punch. And since these techniques cannot be used in these competitions, many of the participants see no reason to train to defend against them.

INTEREST AND FUN

Some people do not do martial arts to win fights or win medals. They just do it because they find the activity fun or interesting. The oriental martial arts in particular are exotic and fascinating. Simply practicing the forms can be a rewarding experience even without any combat application of the moves.

HEALTH AND FITNESS

Some people do martial arts because they believe that it has health benefits. This is quite common among tai chi practitioners many of whom don't really think of it as a fighting art.

Of course, many people do not actually get to make a decision about what to focus on in their martial arts training (though obviously they do get to pick the martial art that broadly matches their requirements as outlined above). Within a martial art, however, the decision of what to focus on is actually made by the instructor and this is almost always predicated on any association that he is operating under. The modern reality of many martial arts is that a major driving force is the grading syllabus. These rules dictate what someone needs to do in order to progress to the next rank and, as is so often the case, their next colored belt. And so, most training will focus on the grading syllabus. In fact, it is becoming more common that students are reluctant and apprehensive about being shown or learning anything else. They tend to not want to waste their time learning anything that is not required for a grading or competition. In real life, however, the opposite is normally true: You can win a fight by knowing something that the other person does not.

Internal and External Martial Arts

External martial arts encourage their students to use big strong moves, confronting every challenge head-on with a tough, aggressive attitude. These martial arts usually encourage the use of "hard" blocks that involve bashing attacks out of the way. Examples of martial arts in this category are karate or kick boxing. An external approach is good because it builds strength of mind and body, and a stronger opponent always has an advantage over a weaker one. It also helps you to overcome problems by training you to struggle against adversity. It is easy for a novice to pick up the external approach because its lack of subtlety makes it simple to understand.

CHARACTERISTICS OF INTERNAL AND EXTERNAL MARTIAL ARTS	
External	**Internal**
Try to change the way things are	Understand the way things are
Struggling	Observing
Hard blocks	Going with the flow
Strong	Fluid
Hard blocks	Soft blocks

Internal martial arts encourage a more subtle approach, using smooth, light movements to slip past attacks or to flow with an aggressor's movements, allowing the internal martial artist to use his opponent's strength against them. Internal arts encourage the use of "soft" blocks that gently direct attacks past the defender. Examples of internal martial arts are aikido and Tai Chi. An internal approach is good because it allows you to fight opponents who are bigger and stronger than you.

Some martial arts tend to emphasize either internal or external skills, but it is very much a personal thing. There are aikido practitioners who have a very external approach to martial arts even though aikido is a very internal art that emphasizes soft blocks and blending with an attack. There are even some internal martial artists who do Shotokan karate, even though the first thing that style does is teach you how to smash incoming attacks out of the way.

There is another terminology that is also used to describe this, and that is of soft and hard for internal and external respectively.

Sparring

If you learn a martial art, it does not necessarily mean that you are learning to fight. There is a lot more to a real fight than just using good techniques. Many of the striking arts practice techniques with imaginary opponents—essentially punching the air. This is great to allow you to learn how to use your muscles to do a particular movement or to learn how to effectively put moves together. However, practicing without an opponent will leave you with a head full of ideas but no practical experience. As a result most martial arts have some sort of sparring, and even within a single martial art there will often be different types of sparring.

> "The weakest of all weak things is a virtue that has not been tested in the fire."
> – *Mark Twain*

1. CONSTRAINED PREDICTABLE SPARRING
This type of sparring follows a predetermined pattern so that both parties know what is coming next. This will usually consist of one person attacking with a predetermined attack, which his opponent then tries to defend against and apply a counter attack. This is mainly useful for developing an understanding of distancing and basic timing.

2. CONSTRAINED UNPREDICTABLE SPARRING
With the addition of an unpredictable element, the ability to react to an unexpected attack is tested, while still constraining the engagement to a single attack so that activity happens in bursts.

3. FREE SPARRING
This kind of sparring is continuous with both partners flowing between an attacking and a defensive role.

Sparring with an opponent will help build skills that are essential for combat and that cannot be developed through solo practice. Ideally, the sparring should be in a competitive environment. This does not necessarily mean an organized competition with a referee and medals, although this does act as a strong motivator for some people. For building up skills, it is better to find a sparring partner whom you trust to test you and stretch your abilities. Sparring with a collaborating partner who is not trying to beat you, letting you succeed where you don't deserve to, has its place for running through drills and getting you familiar with techniques. However, this kind of practice will not provide you with some key skills. Sparring with an opponent who is making a concerted effort to win will build the following skills:

1. Ability to improvise

Having a game plan is great but if things don't go as you expect, then the plan can turn into a trap, constraining you to a set of actions that cannot succeed. When you train using traditional forms everything goes to plan every time because there is nobody there to disrupt your plan.

2. Control over your emotions

In order to perform effectively, you need to have control over your actions. If you lose that control because you are afraid of your opponent then you are going to be unable to act when you need to. If you become angry, then you might act impetuously giving your opponent an opportunity to defeat you. Nobody is afraid of the imaginary opponents in the traditional forms so you need to spar with a variety of live opponents.

3. React under pressure

Being under pressure is subtly different from being afraid of an opponent and in sparring matches the results can be similar, for example, an overly defensive posture and weak, uncommitted, or uncoordinated attacks. Through solo practice you can develop great technical skill but this is of no practical use to you if you crumble under pressure.

4. Use tactics and understand your opponent

Tactics are an important part of any fighting art. It is possible to develop some fundamental tactics without sparring and indeed this is what the standard drills and forms practiced in many martial arts are all about. They are a catalog of tactics that in general are likely to be successful. However, every opponent is different so a stock approach will often not be sufficient. Moreover, the state of an individual is fluid in a fight situation, constantly being updated. Instead, you need to be able to read your opponent to best be able to decide what attacks he is likely to be susceptible to or what actions he is likely make. The ability to gain an understanding of an opponent is best developed by sparring with a variety of opponents.

THE LIMITATIONS OF SPARRING

A sparring activity is unlikely to be popular or productive in the long term if there is a high chance of at least one of the participants getting seriously injured. A variety of approaches have been taken to address the issue of safety. Some martial arts introduced protective equipment such as head guards or gum shields. Even with this protection it is still necessary to have "rules of engagement" limiting which types of attack are allowed, how strong or how fast attacks are allowed to be or defining what areas are legitimate targets. For example, International Taekwondo Federation (ITF) taekwondo and most karate sparring matches are semi-contact fights meaning that participants simulate full power techniques. Attacks are made at full speed but the distance must be controlled so that the motion of the attack is arrested before reaching the target. World Taekwondo Federation (WTF) taekwondo and kyokushin-kai karate on the other hand both engage in full contact contests but do not allow head punches.

Another factor that has shaped how sparring rules have evolved in different martial arts is that of sport. In addition to the safety aspects, for a sparring activity to be successful as a sport it needs to fulfill certain requirements:

(a) should be fun for the participants
(b) should be enjoyable for spectators
(c) there should be a clear winner at the end of it

Protective equipment

For example, in judo contests, a player can be penalized for taking "an excessively defensive posture." Clearly this rule is not about safety but rather about encouraging the contest to progress.

The constraints that sparring rules place on the techniques that are allowed, tend to make the fight less realistic. The restrictions that are the most necessary, those that try to make the sparring activity safe, are rather obviously at odds with the original objective of the older martial arts, which was to try to use attacks that were as devastating as possible. Many martial artists seem to be oblivious to these limitations and think that the way they spar really is how all fights work. Even those who do have some understanding of the contrived nature of their sparring matches can find it hard to override the behaviors that have become hard-wired during their sparring training. The karate man who has trained for years pulling his punches short might find himself doing exactly that in a self-defense context. The WTF Taekwondo man might drop his hands in a fight disastrously leaving himself open to any head punches.

Overall, sparring contests, which should be the solution to the problem of how to train realistically for combat, can end up being part of the problem. This is especially the case when participants fail to understand the implications of the particular rule set that they are following.

Vale Tudo, the Gracie Family, and Mixed Martial Arts

The stylized nature of many of the traditional martial arts can give martial artists a skewed view of reality. Sparring, an activity that should act as a reality check, actually tends to skew this view even further from reality. The fact that most martial arts instructors are convinced of the superiority of their particular style and go to great lengths to impress this on their students makes this even worse. So if traditional martial artists took part in a contest that was closely matched to a real fight, it should be possible for an opponent to exploit these weaknesses. In fact, this is exactly what did happen.

Style versus style bouts started to come to prominence in the 1950s in Brazil where there had, for some years, been a growing sub-culture of fights called *vale tudo* (which in Portuguese means "anything goes"). The rules for these matches varied but usually attacks were fairly unrestricted—typically no eye gouges, groin shots or biting, but otherwise you could do pretty much whatever you wanted, making it very similar to the pankration contests of Ancient Greece. The Gracie family generated a great deal of interest when Carlos Gracie issued the "Gracie Challenge." This challenge defied all-comers to prove themselves against the Gracies, and representatives from a variety of martial arts backgrounds rose to the challenge including karate, boxing, judo, and capoeira practitioners. Carlos Gracie initially issued the challenge as a way to promote his martial art, Gracie Jiu-jitsu, which was based on judo but had evolved into a more practical martial art that placed a particular focus on ground fighting.

What the Gracies realized was that:
(a) Most fights would very quickly end up on the ground
(b) Most fights were decided on the ground
(c) Most martial artists were neglecting ground fighting in favor of flashy kicks or throws

Against opponents with a grappling background, particularly those trained in judo, which traditionally includes a significant amount of ground work, the fights were fairly even. However, against "stand up fighters," that is fighters from backgrounds like boxing and karate, the fights would all go the same way: the Gracie Jiu-jitsu fighter would wait for an opportunity to close the distance and grapple his opponent. He would then bring him to the ground so that he could apply his superior ground fighting skills. His opponent would typically have done no training for ground fighting and so the fight could only end with victory for the Gracie Jiu-jitsu fighter, usually by way of a chokehold.

The success of the Gracies wasn't because they were bigger or stronger than anyone else–Helio Gracie who fought most of the original challenge matches was quite a slight and frail looking individual, certainly by the standards of the world of *vale tudo*. Rather, it was down to superior technique allowing the smaller, lighter fighter to prevail over a heavier opponent.

In 1993, the Ultimate Fighting Championship (UFC) was created. The cross style fights that were shown in the "Gracie Jiu-jitsu in Action" video series inspired this controversial no-holds barred contest. The UFC was televised as a pay-per-view event and dramatically increased interest in what was being called mixed martial arts (MMA). The first UFC fights were with ground fighters, and Royce Gracie won the first few championships. However, MMA quickly evolved as interest grew and the types of techniques required to win these kinds of fights became better understood. Fighters with a background in the striking arts started to achieve better results as they incorporated grappling techniques into their training. Consequently, those with a grappling background started to pay more attention to training that included striking techniques. Overall, the results were that well-rounded fighters started taking part in these types of contest.

Limitations of Ground Fighting

Based on the success of the Gracie family and the success of their ground fighting against other styles of martial art, the logical conclusion to be drawn is that stand-up fighting is a waste of time since fights are going to be won on the ground. However, this conclusion is not correct for all situations. In fact, the situation that ground fighting fails in is that of self-defense, a scenario that is very important to many martial artists.

The typical self-defense scenario is not against a lone trained fighter but is more likely to involve multiple unskilled assailants. Taking an opponent to the ground and then using grappling techniques is effective against a lone opponent, but against multiple opponents it is a very poor tactic. While you restrain one opponent on the ground, you are prone to attack from his friends.

A good example of how to deal with multiple opponents comes from Masahiko Kimura who has been described as one of the greatest Judoka of all time. But he did not only train in Judo – he also practiced karate. It is quite revealing what tactics he used when faced with multiple attackers in 1946:

> The four MP [military police] men surrounded me and took me to the middle of Nagaroku Bridge nearby the station. This was not an ordinary fight to me. I had to win this fight to defend the honor of judo. One of them suddenly threw a right straight at my face. I blocked the punch with my left arm, and kicked him in the groin with full force. He crumbled on the spot. When I turned back my head, another huge MP extended his arms and attacked me trying to grab me from behind. I then hit his right arm hard with knife hand, and then threw him into the river by Seoi-nage [shoulder throw]. The other two were watching this scene in amazement, but charged at me one by one. I delivered a head butt into the face of the third man. He was knocked out. I disposed of the last man by squeezing his balls with full force. Ever since I was in junior high, I have been called Master Groin Squeezer, and had absolute confidence in this technique.

Even though Kimura was an expert in judo, when faced with four assailants he fought more like a karate man, avoiding grappling techniques that would hand over the advantage to his more numerous opponents.

A Complete Martial Artist

Because of the tendency for individual martial arts to focus on particular skills, there is a risk for a practitioner of one martial art to neglect key skills that are necessary to become an all-around fighter. This limitation can be overcome by training in different martial arts that address different elements of combat. At the same time, it is no good to be a generalist who is the jack-of-all-trades but master of none. The most common approach is to initially focus on one martial art, building up an expertise in that approach to fighting, and then to pick up proficiency in a complementary martial art. For example, karate and judo complement each other: karate focuses on striking arts while judo covers grappling and ground fighting.

COMPONENTS OF A COMPLETE MARTIAL ARTIST
Can defend against multiple opponents
Can fight at close range
Knows how to counter grappling attacks
Can fight on the ground
Can defend against an armed opponent

The best fighter is not a boxer, karate or judo man.
The best fighter is someone who can adapt to any style.

~ Bruce Lee

CHAPTER TWO

A Catalog of Martial Arts

Martial arts have had a long history and each culture has had its own martial tradition. This has resulted in a wide diversity of fighting methods. Some martial arts have been developed as cold, practical systems of combat. Others have evolved with a spiritual background with more of an emphasis on self-cultivation than self-protection while some martial arts have been created as sporting activities.

This chapter describes the major martial arts that are popular today.

A brief history of each martial art is given. This provides a background to the kind of thinking that went into the creation of the martial art and what kind of problem was intended to solve. Many of the martial arts are interconnected with one fighting system being adapted to a new way of thinking and giving birth to a new martial art. The history of the martial arts provides an insight into the influences of previous martial arts.

The approach of each martial art is considered, describing how this martial art is taught and practiced, what types of techniques are emphasized, and which are considered unimportant.

Most martial arts have some sort of competition or sport aspect. This is important because good rules add realism while some rules can result in forming bad habits.

For each martial art, a summary of the main styles is given. Within a martial art there is never complete uniformity. Some arts are more like sporting activities and tend to be unified by a common rule system and within such sports there is little variation. In other martial arts, there are many different styles some of which could almost be considered a separate martial art in their own right.

An analysis of each martial art considers the strengths and weaknesses of the art. These considerations are important when deciding which martial arts to cross train in because training in a complementary martial art that focuses on those areas can compensate for the weaknesses in another martial art. For example, Muay Thai omits takedowns and ground fighting while emphasizing striking and so is complemented by judo, which focuses on takedowns and ground fighting while excluding strikes.

A SUMMARY OF THE MARTIAL ARTS PRESENTED IN THIS CHAPTER	
Kung fu	Chinese martial arts with an ancient history
Jujutsu	Japanese grappling art with its roots in the samurai traditions
Aikido	A Japanese grappling art with a Shinto heart
Judo	Japanese grappling and groundfighting art with Olympic status
Karate	Part Okinawan, part Japanese striking art
Kickboxing	Full contact striking sport
Taekwondo	Korean art and Olympic sport that emphasizes kicks
Boxing	Full contact Western sport focusing on punches
Wrestling	Grappling sport
Other martial arts	Some of the many other arts are summarized

Kung Fu

Kung fu (pronounced, and sometimes also written, "gongfu") is usually meant as an umbrella term to refer to the traditional martial arts of China. In fact, the term is even more general than that and can refer to any cultivated skill. A more precise term for Chinese martial arts would be "wushu" but confusingly that term has come to refer to the state sanctioned modern performance sport that is more akin to gymnastics than a martial art. A term that would more accurately describe what is usually meant by kung fu would be "ch'uan fa," which means "way of the fist" and covers the unarmed martial arts of China.

HISTORY

Many accounts of the history of Chinese martial arts point to the Shaolin Temple as the source.

However, China is known to have had a history of martial arts dating back thousands of years, long before the Shaolin temple was constructed. Chinese legends speak of a great general who lived around 2700 BC who wrote extensive manuals on astrology, medicine, and the martial arts. The Confucian text, "Classic of Rites," mentions *jiao li* (the rite of wrestling), which was a grappling martial art developed in the Chou Dynasty (12th-13th Century BC). This martial art consisted of strikes, locks, throws, and made use of the knowledge of vital areas. This eventually became a public sport during the Ch'in Dynasty (221- 206 BC).

The most significant contribution to the Chinese martial arts came from the Shaolin temple. There are many conflicting stories about the origins of martial arts in the Shaolin temple. The legends suggest that at some point in the 6th century, a Buddhist monk from India called Bodhidharma travelled to the Shaolin Temple in China. He discovered that the monks were in too poor a physical state to meditate and pray effectively and so he instructed them in physical exercises to improve their fitness. These exercises became the basis for Shaolin kung fu.

In the Tang dynasty (618-907), the Shaolin temple gained royal patronage after the monks of the Shaolin gave their aid in the Battle of Hulao. This brought a steady flow of pilgrims to the temple, which started to become something of a hub for the exchange of martial arts techniques.

The original Shaolin exercises that are credited to Bodhidharma, called the "Eighteen Hands of Lohan," were taken by a chu'an fa master called Ch'ueh Yuan Shang-jen and combined with movements from his own style, expanding the eighteen hand and foot positions to seventy-two. This was later expanded again to 170 moves after Ch'ueh met another master called Li-shao. These techniques were broken down into five animal forms: Dragon, Tiger, Snake, Panther, and Crane.

In the 20th century, following the fall of the Ch'ing dynasty, the new republican government began to consider its martial arts heritage as a source of national pride. There was a growth in public exposure to martial arts as instructors were encouraged to teach their martial arts. Various national organizations for the martial arts were formed, national examinations were organized and training manuals were published. Demonstration teams were sent overseas, including a demonstration at the 1936 Olympic Games in Berlin.

With the formation of the People's Republic of China in 1949, government attitudes changed radically, with the establishment considering martial arts to be subversive. A new officially sanctioned martial art called modern wushu was devised. Although this new art had the outward appearance of the traditional Chinese martial arts, it was a purely performance art devised by committee and deliberately divorced from any of the traditional styles. The suppression of the traditional arts lead to many of the kung fu masters migrating to Hong Kong, Taiwan, and other parts of the world. This meant that in the 1960s and 1970s, China suppressed its millennia old heritage and entered a dark age for martial arts while the rest of the world experienced a great surge in interest in Chinese kung fu. The Western world experienced a kung fu craze in the 1970s fuelled by "chop socky" movies produced in Hong Kong, in particular the movies of Bruce Lee.

APPROACH

There are such a wide variety of styles of kung fu that it is hard to identify a single approach. However, there are some general trends within the many schools of kung fu.

Kung fu is based around stand up fighting using mainly punches and kicks. It also includes grappling and take down techniques called ch'in na, but often this approach is not emphasized by kung fu schools and ground fighting in particular is usually neglected.

The Chinese martial arts are often broken down into two groups. Northern styles tend to use big powerful kicks, large sweeping movements and high jumps. Southern styles tend to focus on strength and stability using tense immovable stances with fewer kicks.

Many Chinese martial arts emphasize the use of pressure points, which are areas that can be punched, poked, constricted, or otherwise have pressure applied to them in order to produce effects such as pain. Traditional Chinese doctrines often explain these pressure points in terms of energy meridians while more modern explanations concern nerves and blood vessels.

TERMINOLOGY: CHINESE MARTIAL ARTS	
Chi sau	Sticky hands
Kwoon	Training hall
Lap sau	Grabbing hand move
Muk yan jong	Training dummy
Chi	Energy
Sanshou	Free sparring, literally "free hand"
Sifu	Instructor
Wushu	Martial art

AN OVERVIEW OF KUNG FU	
Name	Kung fu
Translation	Achievement through great effort
Country of origin	China
Period of origin	2700 BC
Category	Striking art
Strengths	Fast punches Often includes weapons training Health and fitness
Weaknesses	Grappling and ground fighting usually ignored

Traditional kung fu practice often consists of the following components:

Basics During basic training, students develop the fundamental building blocks of the martial art, throwing punches and kicks and working on developing strong stances.

Forms Most schools of kung fu consider forms to be the most important aspect of the martial arts. Forms consist of prearranged sequences of moves. These can either be solo forms or two-person forms that are practiced with a partner.

Weapons training Some kung fu styles also practice traditional Chinese weapons such as the broadsword, butterfly knives, staff, or the spear.

Wooden dummy Some practitioners use a wooden dummy called the Muk Yan Jong. This usually consists of a vertical post with several horizontal "arms" protruding and various positions. The dummy is used to practice parries against the "arms" and punches and kicks against the central pillar.

COMPETITION

Wushu competitions consist of two categories. In the *taolu* discipline, competitors perform wushu forms, which consist of set offensive and defensive movements. Performances are given scores by judges in a similar way to gymnastics competitions. There are both barehanded forms and weapon forms. In this discipline, famous practitioners include Jet Li who was China's National Wushu Champion five times, and Ray Park who played Darth Maul in *Star Wars Episode I: The Phantom Menace*.

In the *sanshou* discipline, competitors engage in full contact sparring. The rules vary from one tournament to the next. Typically punches and kicks are allowed, including kicks to the legs, and elbow and knee strikes are sometimes allowed. Grappling and throwing is allowed but with a time limit after obtaining a clinch during which a takedown must be executed or the referee will separate the fighters. Joint locks are not allowed. There is no ground fighting: once a fighter ends up on the ground, the fight is stopped and restarted from a standing position. Fights sometimes take place in a roped off boxing ring or it might take place on a raised platform. Sanshou fighters have had a degree of success in various MMA fights, most notably Cung le who defeated MMA veteran Frank Shamrock, breaking Shamrock's arm in the process.

STYLES

There are hundreds of styles of kung fu. A few of the more popular styles are described here.

Wing Chun, which literally means "Spring Chant," is said to be named after the founder of the style, a woman called Yim Wing Chun who was taught ch'uan fa by a Buddhist nun called Ng Mui. Wing Chun favors fast, but somewhat uncommitted attacks over more powerful attacks that might create openings. The idea is to overcome the lack of power by chaining together multiple rapid attacks from close range that overwhelm an opponent. In defense, Wing Chun uses a technique called "sticky hands," which involves maintaining contact with an opponent to gain feedback and quickly react and deflect attacks. The most famous Wing Chun student was Bruce Lee who went on to become a film star and design his own martial arts system called Jeet Kun Do.

T'ai chi ch'uan, which means "supreme ultimate fist" and is meant to embody the ultimate combination of the oriental concepts of the yin and the yang, which represent the positive and the negative forces of the universe. T'ai Chi practice involves slow, smooth movements combined with breath control exercises and is believed to have positive health effects. As a martial art, T'ai Chi places an emphasis on understanding your opponent's center of gravity and uses moves that flow with an opponent's attack combined with "pushing hands" techniques that flow back and unbalance an opponent. T'ai Chi also includes forms that include the use of a weapon, most commonly the broadsword, staff, spear, or fan.

Jeet Kune Do, which means "Way of the Intercepting Fist" is an eclectic martial art created by Bruce Lee. It is also known as "Jun Fan Jeet Kune Do" after Lee's original name, Jun Fan. Lee had originally learned Wing Chun but had become disillusioned with the constraints of the "classical mess" of the traditional form. He borrowed techniques from fencing and boxing but the core idea of Jeet Kune Do was that it should be an approach of how to fight rather than a fixed system of how to do techniques.

Praying Mantis, *T'ang Lang Ch'uan*, is a northern style created by a Shaolin disciple called Wang Lang around 1700. Supposedly inspired by the aggressiveness of the praying mantis and mimics the leg of a mantis with the "mantis hook" hand posture.

Monkey There are many independently created styles of Monkey Kung Fu. It involves taking on the movements and characteristics of a monkey for example, running on all fours and acrobatic movements. Attacks often include open handed slaps and clawing with a semi-closed fist called the monkey paw.

Eagle Claw, *Ying Hsing Ch'uan*, is a Northern style created in the 12th century by General Yue Fei. Joint locks, takedowns, ripping, and gouging moves characterize it.

Choi Li Fut is a Southern style that was created by Chan Heung in 1836. It contains five animal forms: snake, crane, dragon, tiger, and leopard. It is mainly popular in Hong Kong.

Hung Gar is a Southern style named after the Hung family (gar means family) that created it. It was created by Hung Hei Gun in the 18th century combining the best techniques from Tiger style and Crane Style. Hung Gar uses the five animal forms.

Drunken Boxing Also known as *Tsui Chu'an*, literally drunken fist, imitates the swaying and staggering of a drunkard's movements.

ANALYSIS

There are so many styles of kung fu that it is very hard to pin down anything that is generally true about kung fu as a whole. Overall, the trend is that the traditional nature of many of the Chinese martial arts does result in form before function. The moves of kung fu can be very elegant and smooth but at the expense of realism. This is particularly true of styles like Tai Chi Chu'an, which seem useful only for cultivating a healthy mind and body rather than being useful as a practical martial art. Obvious exceptions to this trend are Jeet Kune Do, which was created precisely to move away from these problems and towards a practical fighting method. Also the Sanshou format of fighting is very strong and realistic, using full contact rules and allowing strikes as well as takedowns and the lack of ground fighting is the main limitation.

Jujutsu

Jujutsu is an umbrella term for a wide variety of both ancient and modern Japanese unarmed fighting systems. Jujutsu means "art of softness" reflecting its philosophy of yielding to an attack so that an attackers strength can be used against him. Most jujutsu styles focus on grappling techniques but can also include striking and ground fighting techniques as well as weapons training. Jujutsu practitioners typically wear a heavy cotton uniform called a keikogi (Western practitioners will usually refer to this as simply gi) that consists of wide bottomed trousers and a long sleeved jacket, held together with a colored belt that signifies rank. The keikogi is usually white and a black hakama (a pair of wide pleated trousers) are often worn, though often this is reserved for instructor level practitioners.

HISTORY

The Japanese art of jujutsu has its origins in the martial traditions of the samurai, the Japanese warrior class. The primary weapon of the samurai was a long sword (katana) but the samurai still needed a method for dealing with an opponent when it was impossible, for whatever reason, to use a sword. For example, if the samurai found himself having to fight at very close quarters, then it would be necessary to fight with close range weapons or to fight unarmed. Therefore, this ancient jujutsu was intended to be used on the battlefield against armored opponents. Against this kind of opponent, unarmed strikes such as punches and kicks would be ineffective, so consequently unarmed jujutsu consisted of locks and holds.

During Japan's Edo period (1603-1868), the trend in jujutsu training was less for battlefield use and more for use against an unarmored opponent. Consequently jujutsu styles in this time started to include striking techniques such as punches and kicks, though the emphasis still remained on grappling techniques.

Historically, jujutsu training often included at least some weapon practice, for example the tanto (dagger) or hojo (a restraining cord).

APPROACH

Most jujutsu schools focus on grappling techniques—chokes, joint manipulations, and throws. Practitioners will also learn at an early stage how to fall safely (the art of break-falling) so that they can take part in exercises that involve being thrown while minimizing the risk of injury. Jujutsu is usually taught from the perspective of using it for self-defense. There is an emphasis on staying on your feet rather than on ne waza (ground techniques) because fighting on the ground is sub-optimal from a self-defense point of view (as well as from the battle field point of view from which jujutsu originated).

Jujutsu does include striking techniques (which they call atemi waza) but little focus is placed on these techniques. Usually strikes are practiced just so that they can be defended against or are otherwise considered useful as a distraction before moving in close and applying a grappling technique.

COMPETITION

Competitive jujutsu is a controversial subject. Any competition would need to have rules restricting what attacks can be used but the original spirit of jujutsu was to use every conceivable technique available to win in combat. If you take away these dangerous techniques, then you would be practicing something more akin to judo or karate than jujutsu.

The Romanized spelling "jujutsu" is the most faithful to the Japanese pronunciation of the word and has become the accepted spelling. However, in the past other Romanizations were in common use such as "jiu-jitsu" and its use has persisted somewhat. For example, Brazilian Jiu-jitsu was created at a time when this spelling was common and so is still spelled this way.

However, some forms of competitive jujutsu do exist. One competition format is called "Fighting System" and this consists of three phases. In the first phase, the competitors use controlled punches and kicks to score points. In the second phase, which occurs after a grab has been made, competitors must try to trip or throw their opponent to the mat, with points being awarded based on the quality of the technique. In the third phase, which takes place on the ground, the competitors must try to apply locks, holds, and choke-holds.

Another form of jujutsu competition is called "Duo System." This is a team event in which pairs of competitors from the same team demonstrate self-defense techniques in response to twelve different attacks. Referees randomly call out the attack that must be used, and points are awarded based on the quality of the demonstration.

AN OVERVIEW OF JUJUTSU	
Name	Jujutsu
Translation	Gentle method
Country of origin	Japan
Period of origin	Old-style jujutsu 1300s Edo jujutsu 1600s
Category	Grappling art
Strengths	Wide variety of attacks Defense against a wide variety of attacks
Weaknesses	No realistic contests Lightweight striking practice

STYLES

There have been many different styles of jujutsu over its long history. By the 1800s, there were more than 2000 schools of jujutsu in existence.

Daito-ryu Aiki-jutsu This traces its origins back more than 900 years to a Japanese samurai called Shinra Saburo Minamoto no Yoshimitsu (1045-1127). Daito-ryu was popularized in modern times by Sokaku Takeda in the late 1800s. Daito-ryu was the foundation for aikido, which was created by Morihei Ueshiba who studied under Takeda. It was also the foundation for the Korean martial art, hapkido.

Yoshin-ryu Literally translated as "willow heart school," this style of jujutsu was founded by Akiyama Shirobei Yoshitoki in 1632. Legend has it that his inspiration for the name came about when the founder saw that the branches of the willow tree, unlike other trees, didn't break under heavy snow but instead they just yielded and let the snow fall to the ground.

Tenjin Shinyo-ryu Literally translated this is the "divine true wind school". It was founded by Iso Mataemon Minamoto no Masatari in the 1830s, based on yoshin-ryu. This style of jujutsu was studied by Jigaro Kano, the founder of judo and formed part of the basis for judo.

ANALYSIS

Jujutsu's main strength is that it contains a wide range of grappling techniques while still including a reasonable selection of strikes as well as containing weapon defenses. So, jujutsu does at least address all the phases of combat. However, it doesn't convincingly master any particular area: In the striking phase of combat it cannot match up to the striking arts like boxing, karate, kickboxing, or taekwondo. In the standing grappling phase, judo tends to do better and in the ground phase Brazilian Jiu Jitsu has the edge.

With competition playing only a minor role in the practice of jujutsu, there is always a risk that the attacks that jujutsu practitioners defend against are lacking in realism. Unless you practice against attackers who are making a concerted effort to really hit you then you never know how you would deal with a real situation. However, jujutsu practice is most often with a collaborating partner. It is therefore a good idea for jujutsu specialists to cross train in something like boxing or karate where your opponent will be throwing fast punching combinations that are set up by feints.

Aikido

Aikido is a modern Japanese martial art that focuses on controlling the opponent by way of joint manipulations. Aikido is derived from jujutsu but is unusual in the world of martial arts in that the central idea is to nullify an aggressor while causing him as little harm as possible. The word aikido can be literally translated as "way of harmonizing spirit" and this reflects the spiritual dimension that is considered by many of its practitioners to be central to aikido.

Like jujutsu practitioners, aikido practitioners also typically wear a heavy cotton uniform called a keikogi that consists of wide bottomed trousers and a long sleeved jacket, held together with a colored belt that signifies rank. The keikogi is usually white and a black hakama (a pair of wide pleated trousers) are often worn, though often this is reserved for instructor level practitioners.

HISTORY

Aikido was developed in the 1930s by Morihei Ueshiba who combined techniques from a variety of jujutsu styles, primarily Daito-ryu jujutsu. He also took some of the footwork from sword and spear fighting. Ueshiba was influenced by the idealistic philosophies of the Omoto-kyo religion, which is a branch of the Shinto religion, and he integrated these philosophies into aikido.

In 1931, Ueshiba opened the Kobukan, a dojo (training hall) located in Tokyo, initially calling his art akibudo. In 1942, the Kobukan was closed due to wartime evacuation and Ueshiba moved to Iwama. By this time Ueshiba had moved the focus of his art away from its purely martial roots and more towards a spiritual one. Reflecting this change, he adopted the name aikido for his art.

In later years, the leadership of aikido passed to Morihei's son, Kisshomaru Ueshiba and the Kobukan in Tokyo was reopened. Throughout the 1950s and 1960s, aikido spread to the West and today aikido is practiced throughout the world.

APPROACH

Because of its roots in Daito-ryu, aikido has a great deal of similarity to jujutsu. It focuses on joint manipulations and includes strikes, particularly those against vital areas, mainly as a way of creating openings for a lock or a throw. Break falling is also an integral part of the training.

Aikido is often classified as an internal martial art. One aspect of aikido that helps it to qualify as an internal art is the concept of blending. Rather than use brute force to block an incoming attack, aikido practitioners prefer to try to synchronize their movements with those of the attacker, flowing with the attack and then gently redirecting it. After blending with an incoming attack, the aikido practitioner will usually try to apply a joint lock. The expectation is that in a real live self-defense situation something would break or dislocate. Obviously, during aikido practice inflicting this kind of serious damage to your training partner is not desirable. Consequently the person experiencing the joint lock is also expected to use blending and flow with the lock. This means flipping or rolling out of the lock, which looks very impressive in aikido demonstrations.

The creator of aikido, Morihei Ueshiba, when speaking about the purpose of aikido, said that "to control aggression without inflicting injury is the Art of Peace." One of the central philosophies of aikido is that practitioners should avoid conflict and when attacked they should defend themselves without injuring their opponent.

COMPETITION

Most aikido practitioners do not take part in any competitive fighting matches. The official explanation usually given is that aikido is about harmony and that this is not compatible with the idea of fighting in a competition.

One type of aikido contest is *tanto randori*. One competitor is designated attacker and one the defender. The attacker is armed with a fake knife (usually rubber) and tries to tag the defender with it. The defender must avoid the attacks and is scored on his ability to break the attacker's balance and apply aikido techniques. After a fixed time period the roles are reversed.

Another type of contest is called embu in which competitors demonstrate kata, predetermined techniques, and contestants are scored on their performance.

STYLES

Aikikai This is the mainstream style of aikido and is still controlled by the Ueshiba family.

Yoseikan Aikido Minoru Mochizuki founded this style of aikido in 1931. He integrated techniques from judo and karate in an attempt to create a well-rounded martial art.

KI – An important concept in the eastern martial arts is that of ki (or chi in Chinese martial arts). Ki is best translated as "vital energy" or "life energy" and it has both physical and mental components.

AN OVERVIEW OF AIKIDO	
Name	Aikido
Translation	Way of harmonizing spirit
Country of origin	Japan
Period of origin	1930s
Category	Grappling art
Strengths	Includes a broad range of attacks Defense against weapons as well as unarmed attacks
Weaknesses	No realistic contests Neglects the benefits of going on the offensive

Yoshinkan Aikido This style was created in 1951 by Gozo Shioda. It is noted for its punishing senshusei (expert) course that is used to train Yoshinkan instructors and was originally conceived to help train the Tokyo riot police. Robert Twigger described his experiences of the senshusei course in his book *Angry White Pyjamas*.

Shodokan Aikido Kenji Tomiki created the shodokan style in 1967. The founder decided that what aikido training was lacking was the realism and pressure of sparring with a resisting opponent. Taking ideas that he had learnt from Jigaro Kano, the founder of judo, Tomiki started introducing competitive elements into the aikido training. Shodokan practitioners do not wear hakama as it was found to interfere with safe competitive fighting.

Shin Shin Toitsu Aikido Founded in 1974 by the then chief instructor of the Aikikai, Koichi Tohei. This style of aikido focuses on the application of ki and is often referred to as ki aikido (its governing association calls itself the Ki Society).

ANALYSIS

Aikido practice includes defense against various attacks including punches, grabs, and weapon attacks. It also includes training for defending against multiple attackers. The ability of aikido practitioners to blend with incoming attacks, combined with the fluid counter attacks and the flips and rolls that they cause are very impressive.

However, the emphasis of aikido is to defend against an incoming attack and redirect it rather than to make use of a preemptive attack. While this philosophy is admirable it does means that the initiative is given away to an opponent. This defensive attitude to training can also result in aikido practitioners never really learning how to mount a strong offense. Within such a training environment, a student might only be exposed to other practitioners with the same outlook. This combined with the common rejection of competitions within most aikido schools can mean that an aikido practitioner might never learn to defend against a strong attack. And with all of that blending, you can never really be sure if all those joint locks are really going to work or if the compliant partner is doing all the work with those flips and rolls. Consequently, a common criticism of aikido practice is that these attacks that are thrown are not realistic and are merely caricatures of real attacks and so some doubt is raised as to whether they could successfully defend against a more earnest attack.

Judo

Judo is a modern Japanese martial art and Olympic sport that focuses on grappling techniques and ground fighting. Like jujutsu and aikido practitioners, judo participants typically wear a heavy cotton uniform called a keikogi, or judogi that consists of wide bottomed trousers and a long sleeved jacket, held together with a colored belt that signifies rank. The judogi is usually white but blue uniforms are also common and in many competitions one competitor must wear white and the other blue.

HISTORY

Jigoro Kano created judo, basing it on jujutsu. Kano had studied two styles of jujutsu: *Kito-ryu* and *Tenjin Shinyo-ryu*. Jujutsu practice consisted of step-by-step predetermined moves and Kano felt that this was not sufficient to train someone in how to really fight. He realized that the only way to learn to fight properly was by engaging in free flowing, interactive contests, and so he started to formulate a way that jujutsu could be practiced with a resisting opponent. He called this approach to training randori, which is usually translated as "free practice" (but literally means something like "disordered grasp").

In 1882, Kano founded the first judo school in a Buddhist temple and had just nine members. Over the years, the home of judo, which became known as the Kodokan, would move to progressively larger premises as the popularity of judo grew.

There was a great deal of rivalry between jujutsu schools and the new judo school (at that time it was referred to as Kano's Jujutsu). There were a great many challenge matches between the kodokan and jujutsu fighters. Kano wrote in his memoirs,

"It seemed that the Kodokan had to take on the whole of Japan, and had to have a spirit of being ready for anything."

The turning point came in 1886 when athletes from the Kodokan faced Totsuka-ha Yoshin-ryu jujutsu in a contest organized by the Tokyo metropolitan police. Kodokan Judo dominated the contest, winning 13 out of 15 matches. Judo grew in popularity with new students leaving their jujutsu masters to train with Kano. Ultimately, this would lead to judo displacing jujutsu in Japan.

Kano quickly promoted Judo outside of Japan, travelling to Europe and America in 1889. He became a member of the International Olympic Committee in 1911. Judo was demonstrated at the 1932 Olympic Games but did not become an Olympic sport until the 1964 games in Tokyo.

APPROACH

In formulating *randori*, Kano removed the most dangerous techniques, for example the strikes, whose unrestricted and uncontrolled use would endanger participants. These techniques were preserved in the judo kata, which were rehearsed sequences of moves to be performed in a controlled manner. Thus, there would be two training methods: randori would use a restricted set of moves that could be used without control against a resisting partner; kata would use an unrestricted set of moves to be performed with control against a compliant partner.

Most judo practitioners focus on the competition element and so judo practice focuses on the techniques that are allowed in *randori*: grappling techniques, throwing techniques, and arm locks. Other locks, such as wrist, leg, or spinal locks, as well as small joint manipulations, are not allowed in competition and so tend not to be practiced. Striking techniques only appear in the judo kata and so tend to be overlooked. They are regarded as techniques for advanced students and that their main use is to distract an opponent to allow for close range grappling.

In recent years, there has been a trend towards judo competitors focusing on throws and less on groundwork because throws seem to be more likely to score points in competition.

COMPETITION

Judo is a fully developed sport and is part of the Olympic Games. There is also a judo world championship that is held every two years by the International Judo Federation. Originally there were no weight limits, but over time categories were added and now most competitions have seven weight categories.

There are two distinct phases to a judo fight. During the standing phase, which is considered the initial phase, competitors grapple and attempt to bring their opponent to the ground by way of a throw or a trip. This leads into the ground phase where fighters try to apply a hold, lock, or strangulation. Any time that a point is scored or a penalty applied, the fight is stopped and recommenced in the standing phase.

Points are awarded for throwing an opponent on his back. A perfectly executed technique is awarded an ippon (a full point) and will immediately win the match. If the technique is lacking in some way, for example the opponent lands only partially on his back or the technique is done with less than full force, then there are lower scores that can be awarded but which can be used to determine the winner if no ippon is scored. An ippon is awarded for holding an opponent on the ground for 25 seconds. A partial score is awarded for holding an opponent down for less time than that. An ippon is also awarded if an opponent submits or is incapacitated after being held in an arm lock or strangulation technique.

AN OVERVIEW OF JUDO	
Name	Judo
Translation	Gentle way
Country of origin	Japan
Period of origin	1880s
Category	Grappling art
Strengths	Good ground skills Realistic grappling contests
Weaknesses	Poor against multiple attackers Difficult to use against a heavier opponent Many judo techniques depend on the opponent wearing a judo jacket

STYLES

Brazilian Jiu Jitsu Mitsuyo Maeda originally brought judo to Brazil in 1914, a Japanese kodokan judo practitioner who was a notorious prize-fighter in no-holds barred contests. Maeda taught the Gracie family, who then reformulated and popularized Brazilian jiu-jitsu. They did not use the word "judo" because at that time it was still being referred to as Kano Jujutsu (and due to the conventions of the time it was spelled "jiu-jitsu," which was then a common Romanization). Brazilian Jiu-jitsu, often called Gracie Jiu-jitsu, emphasizes the groundwork aspects of judo. This emphasis has proved the most effective tactic in no holds barred contests and the first Ultimate Fighting Championship (UFC) champion was Brazilian jiu-jitsu practitioner, Royce Gracie.

Sambo This modern Russian martial art is a synthesis of judo, and various regional wrestling styles from China, Armenia, Georgia, Moldova, Uzbekistan, Mongolia and Azerbaijan. Sambo is an acronym for "self defense without weapons."

Notable Sambo practitioners include Vladimir Putin, who is also a 6th dan in judo; Oleg Taktarov who was the UFC champion in 1995; and Megumi Fujii who is an undefeated female MMA fighter and is known as the "Princess of Sambo".

ANALYSIS

The judo philosophy of improving fighting skills through competition is an effective one. It allowed judo to quickly evolve away from its jujutsu roots and almost rendered other similar arts obsolete. However, this came at a cost. While the separation of dangerous techniques into kata allowed safe competition between practitioners, there was a trend towards simply ignoring the kata and the focus was placed on techniques that won competitions.

Judo's status as an Olympic sport brought about an increase in international interest in the art but also had the effect of pushing it further from being a martial art and more towards being a sport. Judo contains a complete ground fighting system but the modern trend in judo emphasizes throws partly because the perception is that these are the techniques most likely to score points in competition.

Karate

Karate, which means "empty hand" is a modern Japanese martial art with its roots in Okinawa. It emphasizes striking, in particular punching and kicking. Karate practitioners typically wear a cotton uniform called a keikogi, or dogi (Western practitioners will usually refer to it simply as a gi). This uniform is similar to the judo uniform but since it does not need to withstand the grappling of judo it is typically a much thinner weave. It consists of wide bottomed trousers and a long sleeved jacket, held together with a colored belt that signifies rank. The keikogi is usually white but some karate schools use other colors.

HISTORY

The island of Okinawa lies in the Ryukyu island chain between China and Japan. It has been strongly influenced by China for centuries and the unarmed martial art native to Okinawa was essentially a local variant of the Chinese "way of the fist," ch'uan fa. In Okinawa this was known as tode, which means "Chinese fist," and in Japanese this is pronounced "karate." Okinawan martial arts were divided between three towns: Naha-te from the port town of Naha, Shuri-te, from the royal city of Shuri and Tomari-te, a small town near to Shuri.

Unarmed martial arts in Okinawa became of greater importance following a weapons ban in 1429 by the King of Okinawa. The Japanese Shimazu clan who annexed Okinawa as a vassal state in 1609 extended this ban. Under these conditions the Okinawan martial arts evolved away from their ch'uan fa roots.

Many of the top practitioners of this Shuri-te were of the Okinawan ruling keimochi class, the most significant of which was Sokon Matsumura who was chief bodyguard to the king of Okinawa. Many of the main styles of karate can trace their lineage back to Matsumura, so in many ways these karate styles are the bodyguard's fighting art.

In 1872, Japan officially annexed Okinawa and abolished the Okinawan ruling class sending the King into exile. As a result, karate masters, who had previously served the king, changed their philosophy, moving away from that of a 19th century royal secret service and more towards an open method of self-defense that would lead to mental and physical self-improvement. Following this new philosophy Anko Itosu, who had studied under Matsumura, introduced karate into elementary schools. He designed new kata, less than half the length of the typical kata, making it more appropriate for teaching to children.

Karate gradually spread to mainland Japan as various Okinawan karate masters travelled to Japan promoting their art. A key figure in bringing karate to Japan was Gichin Funakoshi, who had learned karate from Itosu. He worked on integrating the Okinawan karate, which still had a very Chinese identity. He changed the way that karate was written so that instead of meaning "Chinese hand" it instead meant "Empty hand." He also renamed some of the kata, giving them Japanese names rather than Okinawan or Chinese ones. He also consulted with Jigaro Kano, creator of judo, which was at that time very much established in Japanese culture, and introduced the white uniform and colored belt system from judo.

APPROACH

Karate focuses on using fast straight punches combined with kicks to strike an opponent. Karate practice is broken down into three sections:

Kihon Means basics, involves practicing the fundamental movements, usually punches, kicks and blocks, without a partner.

Kata Meaning forms, involves practicing sequences of prearranged moves. In general, these kata are poorly understood but there is a trend towards interpreting the practical meaning of these forms in what is often called kata application.

Kumite Involves sparring with a partner. These can take the form of formal pre-arranged exercises, typically involving blocking or parrying a punch or kick followed by a counter strike.

Some karate schools also include kobudo, traditional weapons training, with weapons such as the sai (three-pronged dagger), bo (staff), nuchuku (flail), and tonfa (baton).

A central concept in karate is that of *ikken hissatsu*, the one hit kill. This is a concept that seems to have been imported from kendo. A killer blow with a sword hardly stretches the imagination, but in the karate world of the unarmed strike, it is certainly a loftier goal. Even if unrealistic, this aspiration results in practitioners focusing on fast and accurate strikes.

Some karate practitioners develop their punching ability by repeatedly striking a wooden post called a makiwara. Advocates of this training method say that it is a way to develop strong punches with a firm straight wrist as well as conditioning the knuckles to the impact by causing a thickening of the skin. This practice seems to be declining in favor of modern punching bad or sports karate where heavy contact with the fists is avoided entirely.

TERMINOLOGY: JAPANESE MARTIAL ARTS	
dojo	training hall
rei	bow
yoi	ready
hajime	begin
kiai	martial shout
yame	stop
mawate	turn
ippon	one point
wazari	half point
tsuki	punch
geri	kick
uke	block

AN OVERVIEW OF KARATE	
Name	Karate
Translation	Empty hand
Country of origin	Japan (Okinawa)
Period of origin	1800s
Category	Striking art
Strengths	Powerful punches and kicks
Weaknesses	No ground fighting No realistic grappling

STYLES

Shotokan, means "house of Shoto", named after its creator Gichin Funakoshi whose pen name was Shoto. Long low stances and large powerful movements characterize Shotokan.

Goju-ryu, means "hard and soft style" and traces its heritage back to Chojun Miyagi who studied under the Naha-te master Higaonna. Goju-ryu uses a combination of hard linear moves combined with soft circular moves and there is a focus using breathing to improve technique.

Shito-ryu, Founded by Kenwa Mabuni in the 1920s, Shito-ryu is a synthesis of the soft circular styled Naha-te of Higaonna and the hard straight styled Shuri-te of Itosu.

Wado-ryu, Created by Hironori Otsuka in the 1930s, Wado-ryu is a synthesis of Shotokan karate and jujutsu. Wado-ryu, which means "the harmonious way style," combines the linear strikes of Shotokan with evasive maneuvers that involve slipping past attacks. Wado-ryu also focuses on sparring drills that are more complex than the simple block and counter drills of shotokan. These drills, which are called paired kata, include locks and throws reflecting the jujutsu heritage of Wado-ryu.

Kyokushin-kai , was created by Masutatsu Oyama in the 1950s. Kyokushin-kai, which means "ultimate truth school," is based on Guju-ryu karate with some Shotokan influence but places an emphasis on realistic full contact stand up fighting. These full contact fights are done with a minimum of protective equipment, but, as a result, punches and elbow strikes are not allowed to the head. In this way Kyokushin-kai sparring is symptomatic of the realism dilemma within martial arts. In trying to create realism by disallowing head guards while insisting on full contact, the most common attack, the head punch, has been disallowed, resulting in fighters who remain fairly static and make no effort to protect their head. Well known kyokushin-kai black belts include the MMA fighter Bas Rutten and action movie star Dolph Lundgren.

Tang Soo Do, Despite Korean influences and claims of ancient Korean origin, Tang Soo Do remains a Korean version of Shotokan karate. Tang Soo Do means "Way of the Chinese hand," the same as the original characters for karate. The Tang Soo Do hyeong, or forms, are very similar to the Shotokan karate kata and, in fact, Shotokan has more in common with Tang Soo Do than it does with some of the official karate styles such as Goju-ryu. The martial arts legend Chuck Norris began his martial arts career studying Tang Soo Do.

COMPETITION

One type of karate competition is called kumite, which means sparring. It involves competitors attempting to score points by landing punches or kicks on the body or head. In full contact karate matches, these blows are done with full force, but in this case punches to the head are not allowed. In semi-contact karate, head punches are allowed, but all competitors are required to pull their attacks so that they only tag their opponent, thus avoiding injury.

Usually minimal protective equipment is used in these contests. Some contests allow only a mouth guard and a groin guard. Other competitions will require light cotton mitts to be worn that reduce the risk of cuts when punching to the head. Sometimes head protection or shin guards are used.

Another type of karate competition revolves around the performance of ritualized movements called kata, which are scored by judges based on form and concentration.

ANALYSIS

Karate practice focuses most heavily on punching and kicking techniques, usually with the focus on driving forward with these attacks quickly and powerfully. These techniques are usually taught with a great deal of attention to detail, and practice involves many repetitions with the aspiration to develop the perfect technique. As a result karate practitioners tend to be able to strike explosively with millimeter accuracy.

The karate kata contain a number of grappling moves including throws, single-leg take-downs, as well as arm locks and neck breaks. However, karate does not contain any ground fighting techniques, although some of the locks can be transferred to a ground-fighting context, and karate practitioners almost never engage in ground fighting exercises. In a self-defense situation, this makes a lot of sense but it does lead the karate practitioner open to defeat from a skilled ground fighter.

Kickboxing

Kickboxing is a competitive full contact sport that focuses on kicking and punching. Fights are held in a ring and competitors wear boxing gloves and either boxing shorts or long pants with foot-pads, depending on the type of kickboxing.

HISTORY

The origin of kickboxing begins with Muay Thai, which in turn traces its origins back to the ancient art that is now called Muay Boran, which means "ancient boxing" that had been practiced in Siam for centuries. Muay Boran was originally used as a practical fighting art for military and self-defense purposes, but increasingly it became popular as a competitive spectator sport. In the 1920s, a modern set of codified rules were created which became the modern Muay Thai.

In the 1950s Japan, there were two people whose interest in Muay Thai would lead to the creation of kickboxing. A Japanese karate practitioner called Tatsuo Yamada, who had created Nihon Kempo Karate-do, had become frustrated with karate because opponents were not permitted to make full contact. He had taken an interest in Muay Thai and, in 1959, it had inspired him to create a sport that he called "karate boxing" which combined the kicking techniques of karate with the full contact and punching aspects of boxing. At about the same time a boxing promoter called Osamu Noguchi had also become interested in Muay Thai.

Finally Yamada and Noguchi met and worked together to organize karate vs Muay Thai matches. Nuguchi proposed the name kickboxing and the new martial art started to grow in popularity. Noguchi founded the Kickboxing Association in

1967 and the new sport boomed in Japan after being broadcast on television.

In the 1970s, kickboxing spread to North America. At first, fights were organized under various rules since no universal set of rules could be decided. After much political infighting eventually large governing bodies began to coalesce and were able to provide some sort of consistency. However, to this day the International Kickboxing Federation (IKF) and the World Kickboxing Association (WKA) both claim to be the largest kickboxing organizations.

APPROACH

Kickboxers use punches and kicks to damage their opponent. Muay Thai fighters also use elbow and knee strikes. A common tactic in Muay Thai is to hold an opponent in a clinch and then to either to strike the body using knee strikes or to pull the head down while striking up with a rising knee strike.

It is common for kickboxers to use pads as part of their training drills. Focus pads are used to practice light, fast punches as a way of increasing speed and an ability to fire combination punches. Heavy pads are used to practice heavy attacks and to improve the power of kicks and knee strikes. Another type of pad that is used, particularly by Muay Thai practitioners, are thai pads which are a pair of rectangular pads that cover the forearms and can be placed in a variety of positions to allow a sparring partner to practice combinations of punches, kicks, knee strikes, and elbows.

STYLES

Muay Thai, which means Thai boxing, is known as the "Art of the Eight Limbs" because competitors can use punches, elbows kicks and knees. It also allows neck wrestling, whereby an attacker clinches behind the head or neck while throwing knee strikes to the head or body. Well known Muay Thai fighters include Anderson Silva, who has also been very successful in MMA fights.

Muay Boran, which means "ancient boxing" is the predecessor Muay Thai and allows some techniques that are not allowed in Muay Thai fights, such as head butts.

Japanese kickboxing, is based on the fighting system founded by Osamu Noguchi in 1967. The rules are essentially the same as those for Muay Thai, but the point system scores punches and kicks equally which encourages the use of punches more than Muay Thai.

American kickboxing, can be seen as a combination of boxing and karate. Competitors use punches and kicks, but not elbows or knees, and all attacks must be above waist height. Notable American kickboxers include Bill "Superfoot" Wallace" and Benny "The Jet" Urquidez, who went on to star in martial arts movies like *Wheels on Meals* and *Dragons Forever*.

Savate, is a French martial art also known as French Kickboxing that dates back to the 19th century. It allows striking with both the hands and feet, somewhat similar to Muay Thai but knee and elbow strikes are not allowed. Competitors wear boxing gloves and typically these are colored to indicate rank in the same way that a belt does in oriental martial arts.

ANALYSIS

Kickboxing is generally considered a well-rounded and realistic method of stand-up fighting. Muay Thai in particular is very practical and complete because of the inclusion of elbow and knee strikes; practitioners are also familiar with some aspects of

TERMINOLOGY: THAI MARTIAL ARTS	
teh trong	straight kick
teh tud	roundhouse kick
teh glub lang	spinning heel kick
teh khao	axe heel kick
gra-dode teh	jump kick
sok tee	elbow slash
sok tud	horizontal elbow
sok kun	uppercut elbow
mud trong	straight punch
mud wiang san	hook
mud wiang glu	spinning backfist
mud seuy	uppercut

AN OVERVIEW OF KICKBOXING	
Name	Kickboxing
Country of origin	Japan
Period of origin	1920s
Category	Striking art
Strengths	Powerful punches and kicks Full contact fighting
Weaknesses	No ground fighting No take-downs Minimal grappling

the stand-up grappling with clinching and close-range striking. Kickboxing styles such as American kickboxing that do not allow such maneuvers are sometimes criticized as being watered down versions of Muay Thai. However, the gritty realism of Muay Thai has been one of the main barriers to its success outside of Thailand because of its perceived brutality and this has probably led to students favoring American kickboxing.

Muay Thai has gained in popularity as interest in MMA has grown because it is considered an ideal martial art for the stand up striking aspect of MMA and many of the most successful MMA fighters have come from a Muay Thai background. However, Muay Thai has one main weakness in that it does not include any ground fighting. For this reason, kickboxing MMA fighters will always train in another martial art such as judo, wrestling, or Brazilian Jiu-jitsu that covers the takedowns and ground fighting.

Taekwondo

Taekwondo, which means "kick punch method" is a Korean martial art that focuses on kicking attacks. Practitioners wear a white uniform known as a *dobahk* with a colored belt that indicates rank. The *dobahk* is quite similar to the training uniforms of karate and judo but differs in that the top is not a jacket but instead is more of a long sleeved t-shirt. In sparring contests, fighters wear foam head guards and padded trunk protectors.

HISTORY

Korea has a rich history of traditional martial arts, the most popular of which were subak and taekkyeon. However, during the Josean Dynasty (1392-1910) Korean martial arts went into decline. It was not until after the Japanese occupation of Korea (1910-1945) that there was a resurgence of interest in Korean martial arts. By the 1950s, nine kwans (schools) of unarmed fighting had emerged. These were united into one martial art that was named "taekwondo" by Hung Li Choi.

Choi, who is usually referred to as General Choi, is widely regarded as being the creator of taekwondo. Choi had studied both the Korean art of taekkyeon and the Japanese art of karate. He managed to convince the leaders of Korea that taekwondo should be part of the training regime for the South Korean army. In 1966, he founded the International Taekwondo Federation (ITF) and within a few years taekwondo had become one of the world's fastest growing martial arts.

After a series of disputes with the South Korean President, Choi left Korea and moved to Canada. From there he continued to open ITF schools outside of Korea. The response in Korea was to appoint Un-yong Kim in Choi's place. In 1973, Kim created the World Taekwondo Federation (WTF). Choi tried to oppose the WTF by conspiring with North Korea to destabilize the WTF. However, this plan backfired because many of his students and instructors disagreed with these actions and simply switched sides to the WTF.

After years of lobbying by the WTF, taekwondo was accepted as a demonstration sport at the 1988 Games in Seoul and as a full medal sport at the 2000 Games in Sydney.

APPROACH

Taekwondo based its approach on the high power of kicking attacks relative to a punching attack. If you want to break down a door do you punch it down or do you kick it down? Taekwondo practice not only contains a wide variety of kicks but also ways to throw those kicks in combination.

Stretching exercises are an essential part of taekwondo practice because good flexibility is needed to be able to kick effectively.

Breaking exercises are used as part of demonstrations and as requirements in rank tests. This typically involves breaking

TERMINOLOGY: KOREAN MARTIAL ARTS	
dojang	training hall
kyung ye	bow
charyeot	attention
shijak	begin
kihap	martial shout
junbi	ready
keasok	continue
kyoruggi	sparring
kuman	stop
dwiro dora	turn around
jireugi	punch
chagi	kick
makki	block

a wooden board by throwing a punch or a kick at it. Demonstrations often involve other materials such as brick or blocks of ice.

Increasingly the emphasis has been towards pursuing taekwondo as a sport. However, most taekwondo schools still focus on self-defense applications of the art. Often these applications use joint locks in addition to punching but the emphasis is on using the legs for counter strikes, finishing moves, and takedowns.

COMPETITION

WTF competitions prohibit punching to the head and the point system so heavily favors kicks that, from a competition standpoint, there is little point worrying about holding a strong guard. Competitors will try to throw as many kicks as quickly as possible rather than worry about a strong defense. Some competitors also report that blocking a kick can still result in a point being scored against them because many judges use the sound of the impact to indicate a successful attack. Kicks or punches to the body score one point and kicks to the head score two points. The fights are full contact and only full force blows are scored. Knockouts are permitted and result in an immediate win.

The different scoring system used in ITF competitions lead to a different fighting style. Head punches are allowed and competitors will typically hold up a strong guard. Full force blows are not allowed and competitors will be penalized for excessive contact.

ANALYSIS

Taekwondo's focus on an offensive style of fighting that emphasizes kicking produces martial artists capable of impressive and dynamic kicking combinations. This has been one element of the art that has attracted students. However, these techniques are athletically challenging and require a high degree of flexibility to perform, making them inaccessible for those unable to achieve these standards of physical aptitude.

The danger with the taekwondo approach is that it builds an over reliance on kicking techniques. While these are very useful and powerful tools to have in the arsenal, they can prove to be impractical in a real life situation. The fighting style that the WTF competition engenders is highly unrealistic in that it does not allow head punches which, in any real life self-defense setting, would be the most likely attack to have to defend against. Fortunately, most taekwondo instructors realize this and do include defending against such attacks in their classes.

AN OVERVIEW OF TAEKWONDO	
Name	Taekwondo
Translation	Way of kicking and punching
Country of origin	Korea
Period of origin	1950s
Category	Striking art
Strengths	Great variety of kicking attacks Full contact contests
Weaknesses	Close range fighting No ground fighting Some contests ban head punches

Boxing

Boxing, also known as pugilism, is a competitive full contact sport that focuses solely on punching. Competitors wear large padded gloves.

HISTORY

Fist fighting, as a competitive sport, has existed for thousands of years. Ancient Sumerian carvings have been found that depict bare-fisted contests and ancient Indian texts such as the *Vedas*, the *Ramayana* and the *Mahabharata* make reference to fist fighting. Boxing is often referred to as "pugilism," which is a term that dates back to the Etruscans in the 1st Millennium BC.

There were various forms of boxing throughout the Mediterranean in ancient times. Originally, it consisted of bare-fisted fighting, but increasingly fighters would wear leather straps on their hands to protect themselves. Boxing became part of the Greek Olympic Games in 688 BC and was known as *pygme* or *pygmachia*. Boxing existed in the Roman world both as an athletic pursuit as well as a gladiatorial exposition.

In post-classical times, boxing remained popular in various forms throughout Europe. In 18th century England, organized bare knuckle fist fights, then known as prize fights, led to the first bare knuckle champion in 1719, James Figg. Around this time the sport acquired the name of "boxing." In 18th century England, Jack Broughton wrote the first boxing rules, called the London Prize Ring rules, in 1743. Prior to this the sport was very dangerous with no official rules, weight divisions, time limits or referees. Broughton encouraged the use of padded gloves for use in training and demonstrations.

In Victorian times, the practice of boxing came under criticism from the establishment, in particular the clergy and the upper classes. After a particularly brutal 38 round fight that had to be stopped by police, a law was passed, the Anti-Prize Fight Act of 1861, which made it illegal to have any part in a prizefight.

A big step towards the modern form of boxing came about with the creation of the Marquess of Queensbury rules. These rules, drafted in 1865 by John Chambers, were published under the patronage of the Marquess of Queensbury and included most of the elements of modern boxing including a 24-foot square ring, three-minute rounds and a ten second count for fighters who were knocked down.

Boxing was still something of an underground activity and did not achieve legitimacy until the 20th Century with the foundation of boxing commissions and the inclusion of boxing in the modern Olympic Games.

APPROACH

Boxing training includes the following components:

Heavy bag, A boxer's speed, power, and endurance can be improved by punching the heavy bag. One training method is to work on the ability to continue punching at a high intensity for the duration of one round. By having a rest period of the same duration as a boxing match and then returning to the heavy bag, the staying power needed for a boxing match can be built up.

Skipping rope, Using a skipping rope has been a training method in boxing for many years. It can be used to work on endurance, work on being able to develop speed in bursts, and to develop good footwork and rhythm.

Speed ball, Boxers use a small air-filled bag called a speedball or speed bag to improve hand-eye coordination.

Sparring , Sparring can be done in a variety of ways and levels. At the most basic level, sparring practice is essential as a way of getting used to hitting an opponent and of being hit while also building endurance. More advanced boxers use sparring to build up tactics and ring craft.

STYLES

The following fighting styles are commonly used by boxers:

Brawler/slugger, The brawler is like a tank, relying not on finesse but on sheer power. They favor single powerful punches over combination punches. Brawlers typically are not very mobile but instead are good at absorbing punches. Famous Brawlers include Sonny Liston and George Foreman.

In-fighter/swarmer, The in-fighter tries to stay close to their opponent, putting them under pressure with a flurry of attacks. This type of fighter uses aggression to put his opponent on the back foot, and bob and weave maneuvers to close the distance without being hit. Famous in-fighters include Mike Tyson and Joe Frazier.

The Marquis of Queensbury Rules

1. To be a fair stand-up boxing match in a 24-foot ring, or as near that size as practicable.

2. No wrestling or hugging allowed.

3. The rounds to be of three minutes' duration, and one minute's time between rounds.

4. If either man falls through weakness or otherwise, he must get up unassisted, 10 seconds to be allowed him to do so, the other man meanwhile to return to his corner, and when the fallen man is on his legs the round is to be resumed and continued until the three minutes have expired. If one man fails to come to the scratch in the 10 seconds allowed, it shall be in the power of the referee to give his award in favor of the other man.

5. A man hanging on the ropes in a helpless state, with his toes off the ground, shall be considered down.

6. No seconds or any other person to be allowed in the ring during the rounds.

7. Should the contest be stopped by any unavoidable interference, the referee to name the time and place as soon as possible for finishing the contest; so that the match must be won and lost, unless the backers of both men agree to draw the stakes.

8. The gloves to be fair-sized boxing gloves of the best quality and new.

9. Should a glove burst, or come off, it must be replaced to the referee's satisfaction.

10. A man on one knee is considered down and if struck is entitled to the stakes.

11. No shoes or boots with springs allowed.

12. The contest in all other respects to be governed by revised rules of the London Prize Ring

Out-fighter, The out-fighter attempts to keep distance between himself and his opponent. These fighters will try to use long-range attacks, typically the jab, to hit without allowing their opponent to counter, often employing superior footwork to maintain the advantage. the most well known out-fighter was Muhammad Ali.

Boxer/puncher, A puncher is well-rounded fighter, similar to an out-fighter using mobility to fight at a distance, but they are also able to close the distance and wear down their opponent using combinations. Examples of well-known punchers are Sugar Ray Robinson and Joe Louis.

COMPETITION

Amateur boxing, This form of boxing is used in the Olympic and Commonwealth Games. It focuses more on technique than power, with points being awarded for clean punches delivered to the head and body. Participants wear head guards. Matches have only a small number of rounds, usually three or four. Many amateur boxers go on to become professional boxers. The Olympics in particular has been a pipeline to the world of professional boxing and gold medalists Cassius Clay (later known as Muhammad Ali), Joe Frazier, and George Foreman all went on to become Heavyweight Champions of the World.

Professional boxing, In professional boxing, strength and endurance are as important as skill. Head protection is not permitted in professional boxing and matches are longer than amateur matches, usually 10 or 12 rounds long.

BOXING TERMINOLOGY	
Chin	Ability to withstand punches
Glass jaw	A fighter who can easily be knocked out
Hammerhead	A fighter who can take punches without getting knocked out
Orthodox	Fighting with the left leg forward
Southpaw	Fighting with the right leg forward
KO	Knockout – a fighter is rendered unconscious
TKO	Technical knockout – a fighter is judged too injured to continue fighting
makki	block

AN OVERVIEW OF BOXING	
Name	Boxing
Country of Origin	England
Period of origin	1867 (in its modern form)
Category	Striking art
Strengths	Full contact contests
Weaknesses	No grappling No kicks No ground fighting No weapon defenses

ANALYSIS

Boxing is unsurpassed for punching technique and is an overall great way to practice stand-up fighting. The highly competitive and full contact nature means that techniques and tactics that do not work are quickly exposed. However, when viewed alongside the entire catalog of martial arts it can seem very one dimensional, entirely neglecting kicking, grappling, or ground fighting.

Wrestling

Wrestling is a broad term covering fighting styles that use grappling techniques to control or make an opponent submit. There are many different styles of wrestling from all over the world and most have long histories. Wrestling has two main forms. Firstly, it is a competitive sport that is included in the Olympic Games and is most commonly practiced at college and high school level in the United States. Secondly, it is a form of entertainment called professional wrestling in which fights are choreographed in advance. In amateur matches, competitors wear a singlet and wrestling shoes and may also wear kneepads. In professional wrestling, there are no restrictions on what the participants may wear and a wide variety of costumes are worn, as a way of increasing the entertainment value.

HISTORY

The practice of unarmed grappling dates back to ancient times with records of wrestling matches in the ancient texts of various cultures. In India, The *Mahabharata* contains a wrestling match in which the combatants "with bare arms as their only weapons ... grasped and struck each other." The ancient Sumerian text, The *Epic of Gilgamesh*, describes a wrestling match between Gilgamesh and Enkidu, saying that "they grappled, holding each other like bulls ... Gilgamesh bent his knee with his foot planted on the ground and with a turn Enkidu was thrown." Evidence in the shape of artwork on pottery, coins, and friezes indicates that wrestling was popular in both ancient Greece and Egypt.

Wrestling became an event in the ancient Olympic Games and after the conquest of Greece by the Romans, wrestling became absorbed into Roman culture.

The modern form of Greco-Roman wrestling was formulated in the 19th Century and was popular throughout mainland Europe, while freestyle wrestling became popular in the United Kingdom and the United States. Wrestling was popular first in fairs and carnivals, and then, as gymnasiums and athletic clubs grew in popularity, regulated competitions with more formal rules were organized. In the 20th century, Greco-Roman wrestling became part of the modern Olympic Games and, in later years, freestyle wrestling was included.

Prior to the First World War, carnival show prizefights had few rules and were very popular. This kind of wrestling died out and was replaced by two types of wrestling: "shoot" in which fighters actually competed to win and "show" in which matches were mere spectacle.

APPROACH

The objective of the wrestler is to either pin his opponent or to apply a painful lock that will force him to submit. In general, strikes of any kind are forbidden in wrestling although, as a hybrid style, shoot wrestling often includes some strikes. Pro wrestling also includes certain strikes but these would be theatrical attacks.

STYLES

Greco-Roman, is a type of amateur wrestling and is included in the Olympic Games. It was formulated in France in the 19th century but follows in the tradition of ancient Roman and Greek wrestling. It does not allow the use of legs to apply a hold, nor does it allow any holds below the belt. Throws are allowed but trips are not.

Freestyle, is similar to Greco-Roman wrestling in that it is an amateur style that is included in the Olympic Games. Unlike Greco-Roman, it allows the use of the legs to apply holds as well as allowing certain locks to be applied to an opponent's legs.

Catch, the term catch wrestling is derived from the Lancashire folk wrestling style "catch-as-catch-can", which is one of its major influences. Another influence was the American folk wrestling style, which was known as rough and tumble fighting. Catch wrestling formed the basis for many hybrid-fighting systems, including Sambo and MMA. Well-known catch wrestlers include Frank Shamrock and Ad Santel (who once, after defeating the then judo champion, declared himself World Judo Champion).

WRESTLING TERMINOLOGY	
Contact	This indicates that the wrestlers must initiate contact
Dawai	An indication to wrestle more actively
Defaite	An opponent has been defeated
Head up	This indicates that a wrestler must lift his head and this warning is given when a wrestler repeatedly attacks by thrusting his head forwards
Jambe	In Greco-Roman wrestling, this indicates that a leg has been used or grabbed
Ordered hold	A specific starting hold used in freestyle as a tie-breaker and in Greco-Roman to initiate the par terre phases.
Par terre	Grappling on the ground
A terre	Instruction given to continue a bout on the ground
Out	A hold was applied outside the mat area
Touché	A wrestler was beaten by a fall

AN OVERVIEW OF WRESTLING			
Name	Wrestling		
Country and date of origin	Greco-Roman	Europe	1800s
	Shoot	Japan	1970s
	Freestyle	USA	1900
	Professional	USA	1860s
	Catch	USA	1900
Category	Grappling art		
Strengths	Good ground skills Realistic grappling contests		
Weaknesses	Poor against multiple attackers Difficult to use against a heavier opponent No weapon defenses Multiple opponents not considered		

Professional, wrestling has its roots in carnival sideshows in the 19th century and is more of a form of entertainment than a competitive sport. It does contain elements of catch wrestling and includes grappling and striking techniques, but it is mock combat with choreographed moves and prearranged outcomes. Many pro-wrestlers have achieved a celebrity status, for example Hulk Hogan and The Rock.

Shoot, wrestling covers a variety of hybrid fighting systems that were developed in Japan in the 1970s. Shoot wrestling is based on freestyle and catch wrestling but with influences from judo, Muay Thai, and karate. The different shoot wrestling systems, such as Shooto and Pancrase, have various rules but typically allow certain strikes while the focus is on grappling with the objective of accomplishing a submission hold.

COMPETITION

International amateur wrestling competitions are organized by FILA (Fédération Internationale des Luttes Associées). There are four types of competitions: freestyle, Greco-Roman, women's wrestling, and beach wrestling. There are a variety of age and weight categories. Fights are conducted within a circle with a diameter of nine meters. Bouts are divided into three periods, each of two minutes in duration, and a match is won by the winner of two periods. Points are awarded for throwing an opponent, with more points given if an opponent lands on his back. Greco-Roman periods are formally divided into a standing phase of one minute followed by two 30-second phases "par terre," on the ground. There are many restrictions on the types of techniques that are allowed, for example strangulations are forbidden as are many arm locks. In Greco-Roman wrestling, no holds that grab or use the legs are allowed.

ANALYSIS

Wrestling contains a wide variety of grappling techniques, and wrestlers are very effective at fighting on the ground. Wrestling is aimed at competition fighting rather than self-defense and so offers no specific defenses against weapon attacks or multiple attackers. While a major component of wrestling involves technique, strength is a major factor, and so it is difficult for a wrestler to compete against a bigger and heavier opponent. For those who view a martial art as a way of overcoming a bigger opponent, this could be viewed as a drawback.

Wrestling has proven to be a valuable skill to MMA fighters and many wrestlers have successfully competed in MMA competitions, for example Randy Couture, Ken Shamrock, and Frank Shamrock.

Mixed Martial Arts

Mixed Martial Arts (MMA) is a full contact sport that uses a wide variety of techniques combining the use of strikes with grappling skills, including fighting on the ground. Fighters wear shorts and fingerless "MMA" gloves.

HISTORY

In a way MMA is one of the most modern martial arts. The term "mixed martial arts" only really coming into common usage in the 1990s. Dedicated MMA gyms only came into existence in recent years, and most of the top practitioners have come into MMA having first learnt fighting techniques from martial arts such as kickboxing, Brazilian Jiu Jitsu, or wrestling. However, in other ways MMA is one of the oldest martial arts in that it is in many ways identical to the ancient Greek full contact sport, *pankration.*

There has long been an interest in the idea of no holds barred fights: In Europe and in the USA, catch wrestling was popular as a carnival show during the late 19th and early 20th centuries; in Brazil, underground fights known as *vale tudo*, meaning anything goes, were popular in the early 20th century and out of this culture came the Gracie family's challenge matches that pitted fighters from a variety of martial arts against the Gracie family and their style of jiu-jitsu; in 1970s Japan, a wrestler called Antonio Inoki hosted a series of matches against fighters from a variety of martial arts, including one against Muhammad Ali.

The first MMA organization was Shooto, created in 1985 by Satoru Sayama (also known as "Tiger-mask"). However, Shooto matches could not really be considered MMA until 1994, when it first allowed striking. Continued interest in MMA in Japan lead to the creation of the PRIDE Fighting Championships in 1997.

In 1993, the Ultimate Fighting Championship (UFC) was created based on Brazilian *vale tudo* and was shown as a pay-per-view event. The original format included very few restrictions on what fighters could do and this quickly led to accusations of brutality. Political pressure eventually led to UFC embracing stricter rules. In 2000, the Unified Rules of Mixed Martial Arts were created and these are now considered the de facto standard MMA rules in the United States.

AN OVERVIEW OF MIXED MARTIAL ARTS (MMA)

Name	MMA
Translation	Mixed Martial Arts
Period of origin	Late 20th Century
Category	Striking and grappling art
Strengths	Full contact contests Balances and integrates different skills
Weaknesses	No weapon defenses Multiple opponents not considered

APPROACH

There are a number of approaches that MMA fighters use during a fight. Fighters will often have a preference about which approach to use, often depending on their background. For example, fighters from striking arts like karate or Muay Thai will typically prefer a sprawl and brawl approach that allows them to make use of their strikes.

Sprawl and brawl, This approach involves fighting from a standing position and throwing punches and kicks. A fighter using this approach will usually try to counter takedown attempts by using a sprawl so that they can return to the stand up phase of combat.

Clinch fighting, A clinch fighter will attempt to close the distance to his opponent and then hold them in a clinch. From the clinch he will use close range strikes like elbow and knee strikes.

Ground and pound, This approach involves taking an opponent down to the ground and then trying to adopt a dominant position from which he can throw strikes down on his opponent.

Submission grappling, This involves grappling with an opponent and attempting to use a submission hold such as an arm lock or a chokehold.

COMPETITION

UFC, The Ultimate Fighting Championship (UFC) is a USA based promotion that uses the Unified Rules of Mixed Martial Arts. Fights take place in an eight-sided caged enclosure called the Octagon.

PRIDE, The PRIDE Fighting Championships (or PRIDE FC) was a Japanese MMA event that began in 1997. The promotion was acquired in 2007 by the Zuffa, who own rival UFC, and resulted in PRIDE being discontinued.

K-1, combines the rules of various stand-up fighting styles. It primarily organizes fights in Japan. K-1 fights are banned in most U.S. states.

Pancrase, is an MMA promotion run by the Japan-based Pancrase Hybrid Wrestling organization. The name of pancrase is derived from the ancient Olympic pankration event. Pancrase came from a professional wrestling background and so originally its rules reflected this. Punching with a closed fist is banned in favor of palm strikes. Recently, the Pancrase promotion has changed its rules so that they are more in line with UFC/PRIDE.

ANALYSIS

MMA fights are full contact and allow a wide variety of strikes and grappling techniques. As such, it is probably the most realistic fight form in existence. MMA competitions have quickly helped establish what works and what does not work. However, the MMA format typically disallows the most dangerous techniques and a complete martial artist should know how to use these as well as how to defend against them. MMA also does not prepare a fighter to defend against an attacker with a weapon. The typical MMA tactics are designed for use against a single attacker, and the typical MMA techniques that are executed during ground fighting can leave a fighter vulnerable if fighting multiple opponents.

Other Martial Arts

There are many other martial arts in the world. Here are a few of the most important ones.

CAPOEIRA

Capoeira is an Afro-Brazilian martial art, which primarily consists of sweeps, kicks, and feints connected by fluid acrobatic movements. Capoeira is usually practiced as a folk dance with participants playing musical instruments and singing while pairs take turns sparring.

ESKRIMA

Eskrima is a family of Filipino martial arts (FMA) that focus on stick and sword fighting, and is also known as *Kali* or *Arnis de Máno*. Eskrima practitioners, called *eskrimadors*, usually fight with two rattan sticks or with a stick and a dagger. Eskrima is generally considered to be one of the best martial arts for learning knife defenses.

FENCING

Fencing is a European martial art and Olympic sport that involves fighting with the sword. Fencing dates back to the 14th century and originally was concerned with a variety of weapons including the dagger, spear, and poleaxe as well as the sword. Currently there are three fencing weapons: the foil, a light thrusting weapon; the épée, a thrusting weapon that is heavier and more rigid than the foil; and the sabre, a light thrusting and slashing weapon. Fencers wear a protective jacket reinforced with kevlar, a protective gauntlet for the sword arm and a mask with bib that protects the head and neck. An electrical system is used to register scoring hits.

KRAV MAGA

Krav Maga is an unarmed fighting style, developed in Israel and adopted by the various Israeli security forces. Krav Maga is Hebrew and means "contact combat." It is designed to be used against potentially lethal threats including opponents armed with knives or firearms and uses the approach that practitioners should train under adverse conditions, for example in difficult terrain, in bad visibility, or while being distracted.

HAPKIDO

Hapkido is the Korean cousin of Aikido and is derived from daito-ryu aiki-jutsu. Yong Sul Choi founded it in 1940 by combining aiki-jutsu techniques with taekwondo. The result was an impressive looking martial art that includes the flowing wrist and arm locks of aikido and the dynamic flying kicks of taekwondo. Some Hapkido schools include training in traditional weapons such as the sword, nunchuku, rope, and staff.

IAIDO

Iaido is a Japanese sword art. It involves the drawing of the sword, cutting with the sword and cleaning and returning the sword to the scabbard. Iaido emphasizes smooth, precise movements and in particular the drawing and cutting actions are executed as one continuous motion. Iaido is usually practiced as a solo activity but some styles include partner work.

KENDO

Kendo is the Japanese art of sword fighting. Practitioners fight using bamboo sticks called the shinai and wear armor protecting the upper body, a masked helmet to protect the head and heavy gloves to protect the hands. Kendo emphasizes an offensive attitude and focuses on strong counter strikes in response to an opponent's attack instead of focusing on blocking or parrying.

NINJUTSU

Ninjutsu, meaning "stealth techniques," is the martial art of the shinobi who are popularly known as the ninja. Ninjutsu covers a wide range of infiltration, survival, and fighting skills but modern practitioners usually focus on unarmed combat and some weapons training such as sword fighting.

SUMO

A Japanese sport in which competitors attempt to either push their opponent out of a circular ring or to drop them to the ground. In addition to grappling skills, body weight is a major factor in sumo contests and competitors are renowned for their large body mass.

Sound, calm mind.
Be light in body.
Have a clever mind.
Master the basics.
~ Gogen Yamaguchi

CHAPTER THREE

Combat Basics

There are some common concepts that are useful in martial arts, and this is re-gardless of the martial art in which you are specializing. For example, knowing that there are different phases to a fight; namely, the striking phase, the grap-pling phase, and then ground fighting is useful to put your own training into perspective. Also, all the techniques that you learn or come across in your train-ing will be applicable to a particular range, which is useful when your opponent is a certain distance away from you.

Phases of Combat

A fight can be broken down into three phases, the striking phase, the grappling phase, and the ground-fighting phase. Real fights will quickly end up on the ground, unless within the striking phase you either knock out or deter your opponent sufficiently from continuing the fight. These phases of combat are useful in thinking about where your strengths and weaknesses lie within your training and knowledge. A karate or kung fu person will be strong in striking techniques and weak in grappling and ground fighting. Conversely, a judo, aikido, or jujutsu person will be strong in the grappling and ground-fighting phase and weaker in the striking phase.

1. STRIKING PHASE
The striking phase is where you are standing up and mobile. You are not in constant contact with your opponent, but you are attempting to throw strikes against each other. You may attempt, particularly if your strength is in a grappling art, to transition from this phase to the grappling phase while avoiding being hit as you try to close the distance. If you are more of a striking specialist, then you might maintain at a distance to continue fighting with strikes. The striking phase can be sub-divided into two ranges: kicking range where you are too far to easily hit with a punch but can reach with your longest weapons, your legs; and punching range where you can hit with jabs, crosses, hooks, and uppercuts.

2. GRAPPLING PHASE
In the grappling phase, you are close to your opponent and possibly have him in a clinch. From this range, you can throw close range striking techniques such as knee or elbow strikes. You can attempt to transition to the ground phase by using a throw or some other takedown. If you are a striking specialist, then you might try to break any hold that your opponent has on you so that you can return to the striking phase.

3. GROUND FIGHTING PHASE
In the ground fighting phase, you are on the ground in contact with your opponent. In this position, you can attempt to acquire a submission hold such as an arm lock or choke hold. It is possible to use strikes such as punches, elbow strikes, and knee strikes during ground fighting, particularly if you are in a dominant position such as a mount or a side control position.

Fighting Ranges

All attacks and defenses have their optimum operating range. For an opponent that is far from you, your best attacks will be kicks because your arms will not be able to reach. As opponents close in on you, they will come into your punching range. Closer than that, and you are into grappling range from which you can use your shortest ranged strikes using your elbows and knees. From there, some form of a takedown move will lead you into the ground fighting phase and again another different range for your techniques.

Which technique you use will depend on the proximity of your opponent. So it is important to bear this in mind when training so that you can think of appropriate situations and applications for these moves.

Kicking range

Punching range

Grappling range

Takedown

Ground fighting

Target Areas

An attack to any part of the body can cause pain and even injury to your opponent. Hit a particular target area, and your attack will have been even more effective. The martial arts have a number of target areas that are attacked. These are particularly vulnerable areas of the body where an attack will be even more devastating. In general, attacks to these target areas can cause injury, loss of consciousness, or even a fatality.

Crown — A strike to the top of the head, for example with an elbow strike, can cause unconsciousness.

Eyes — A finger jab to the eye is one of the most devastating attacks. Even just feigning to the eyes will cause a reaction. Even a slight strike to the eye will cause temporary or even permanent blindness.

Temple — The skull is thinner at the temple. A strike here can result in disorientation or unconsciousness.

Nose — Striking the nose, especially from the side, can cause a painful break and will make the eyes water, reducing vision. Striking upwards under the nose will lift the head allowing for follow up attacks. A heavy strike may cause cartilage fracture.

Ears — A strike to the ear can cause disorientation and pain. This is particularly effective if done with a flat hand. A heavy strike can cause damage to the inner ear.

Jaw — A hit under the chin will lift the head allowing for follow-up attacks. A heavy blow can result in a knockout. A strike to the side can lead to a broken jaw.

Throat — Applying pressure to the throat using a chokehold can restrict breathing, which will eventually lead to unconsciousness. A heavy strike to this area can crush the windpipe leading to serious injury or death.

Carotid Artery — A strike to the side of the neck can cause pain and can have a stunning effect. A heavy block can result in a knockout.

Clavicle — A strike to this bone can cause it to break, causing pain and disabling the arm.

Solar plexus — A strike to the solar plexus will wind an opponent by causing the diaphragm to spasm making it difficult to breathe.

Floating Ribs — A heavy blow can result in broken bones.

Kidneys (by attacking the back) — A strike to the kidneys causes pain. A heavy blow can cause internal injuries and death.

Elbows — An arm lock can be applied by hyperextending the elbow.

Forearm — A strike to the forearm mound can cause pain and numbness in the arm.

Wrists — A hyperflexing wristlock can be applied by bending the wrist beyond its natural range of motion.

Fingers — The fingers are very fragile. Small joint manipulation can be very painful.

Groin — A strike to the groin, whether a knee, a kick or even a punch will cause intense pain.

1. Crown
2. Eyes
3. Temple
4. Nose
5. ears
6. Jaw
7. Throat
8. Carotid Artery
9. Clavicle
10. Solar plexus
11. Floating ribs
12. Kidneys
13. Elbows
14 Forearms
16. Fingers
17. Groin
18. Stomach
19. Thigh
20. Knees

Stomach — If the muscles are tense then this normally has no effect. A strike against an opponent who either is not ready or hasn't got strong muscles can knock the wind out of them.

Thighs — A strike to the thigh, for example with a kick or knee strike, will cause pain and will disrupt an opponent's stance. A heavy blow or repeated blows will cause an opponent to collapse.

Knees — A strike to the kneecap can result in a dislocation. A strike to the back of the knee, for example with a roundhouse kick, will disrupt an opponent's stance and can cause a loss of mobility.

Line of Attack

A useful concept to have in mind during your training is the line of attack and defense. When you are facing your opponent, as a beginner, you are likely to only move forwards and backwards in line with your opponent when attacking and defending. As you progress, you can start coming off the line. This is a useful technique for avoiding attacks completely and letting your opponent go past you so that you can then place an attack on the side of their body. To start with, they may not be defending in that direction. Being light enough on your feet to move around fluidly and to change your line will make you a more difficult target for your opponent, while potentially increasing your chances of a successful attack of your own.

Reflex Training

Martial arts use numerous repetitions of techniques in their training regimen. The idea is that this will then help you to have reflexive actions to attacks in order to block or take advantage of openings. There are a few stages that you can work through as you try to develop these reflexive responses:

1. Slow and predictable—to ensure that you understand the move and that you are performing it accurately.
2. Fast and predictable—now that you naturally execute the move correctly, you can speed the action up and train towards performing accurately at speed.
3. Slow and predictable with a partner—this time you practice the move, while your partner works with you by supplying the attack that you are blocking or by defending against your attack.
4. Fast and predictable with a partner—now that you have mastered performing the move at a slower speed, you can work with your partner to practice the move in a simulated live environment.
5. Slow and unpredictable with a partner—Now you can work towards mastering this move in a more unpredictable environment by working with your partner in a more freestyle format. Here you can vary the timing of the moves and also use combinations to put the move you are practicing within a sequence.
6. Fast and unpredictable with a partner —This is ultimately what you are aiming for and is the closest simulation to real life. Here you work with your partner at full speed.

Basic Combat Techniques

There are number of basic combat techniques that are used throughout the later chapters in this book. They often form part of the starting position for numerous moves described in this book. For this reason, they are described here in detail.

FIGHTING STANCE

While in the striking phase of combat, you need to remain mobile so that you can attack or avoid attacks. The fighting stance is useful for ensuring that you position yourself so that you can do just that.

- The legs are slightly bent and relaxed. You want to be as light and as mobile on your feet as possible.
- You should stand on the balls of your feet, as this enables you to move faster than if you were standing in a flat-footed position.
- Your upper body should be angled roughly sideways on to the direction you are facing. This makes it more difficult for an opponent to land an attack squarely onto your body. This position should mean that any blows directed to that area are more likely to be glanced off.
- You should keep your arms in front of you ready to strike, to block attacks, or to grab your opponent.
- Your leading hand should be slightly more raised than your rear arm. This way you can use your front arm to deflect or block any incoming attacks to the head.

Fighting stance

Fighting stance using a low guard

Make a fighting stance by standing with your left foot about a half step ahead of your right. To maintain mobility, try to keep your weight more on the balls of your feet rather than on your heels. Place your right fist alongside your chin, with your elbow pointing down and protecting your ribs. Keep your right fist in front of you at head height.

Usually right-handed fighters will stand with their left leg forward and left-handed fighters will stand with their right leg forward (which boxers call "southpaw"). Some martial arts encourage the ability to use either side interchangeably.

An alternative form of the fighting stance uses a low guard. The forearm of your leading arm will act as a defense against attacks thrown at your body and ribs. So make sure that your elbow points downwards to enable this. The high guard is usually used in situations where it is a priority to protect the head, for example in full contact fights such as Boxing and MMA where a head strike can result in a knockout. The low guard is more common in competitions where defending the head is less important, for example in WTF taekwondo or kyokushin-kai karate where head punches are not allowed or in other styles of karate where attacks to the body score equally to attacks to the head.

BASIC GRIP (HOLD)

The basic grip is useful when in the grappling phase. This grip is a way of holding your opponent as you prepare to then execute another move. It is commonly used as a starting position for throws. It allows you to respond to attacks from your opponent and also to initiate throws of your own.

The basic grip is only useful if your opponent is wearing a garment suitable for grabbing, for example a heavy weight jacket like the judo training uniform. In judo, gripping techniques are called *kumikata*. If their clothing doesn't have sleeves, you can hold onto their wrists. However, if they don't have anything to hold onto near their neck then it can be difficult to find a strong enough area from which you can execute a throw.

Stand with your right leg forward. With your left hand, grab your opponent's right sleeve. With your right hand, grab the lapel of your opponent's jacket. You are now ready to initiate your next move.

Note that in this position, your opponent's arms and legs are still free and so they are able to attack you. This is fine if you are just practicing throws or are in a judo fight where strikes are not allowed but in other situations you will need to transition quickly to a more secure position like a clinch.

CLINCH (HOLD) – SINGLE COLLAR TIE

A clinch, also known as a tie-up, is a hold used in the grappling phase of combat to control an opponent. A clinch is used to stop an opponent from moving away or striking effectively and can also be used as a precursor to a takedown. The simplest clinch hold is the single collar tie.

Step 1 *To hold your opponent in the single collar tie, place your hand behind your opponent's head.*

Step 2 *Your opponent is then most likely to match your hold with a clinch of his own. In this case, keep a tight hold on his clinching arm in the crook of his elbow. Keep your head close to his shoulder to avoid him pulling your head down into any knee strikes.*

CLINCH (HOLD) – DOUBLE COLLAR TIE

The double collar tie is commonly used in Thai boxing, so much so that it is often called the Muay Thai clinch. It also sometimes called the necktie or plum position.

To hold your opponent in the double collar tie, place both of your hands behind your opponent's neck.

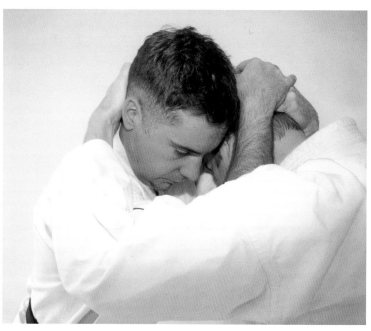

Your opponent will try to do the same but you need to make sure that you have your arms on the inside and with your opponent's arms on top.

If you wish to escape from a clinch and transition back to the striking phase of combat then you can use your knee to push in and collapse your opponent's stance.

One way to defend against these attacks while in a clinch is to place one arm across to the opposite arm protecting your face. The double collar tie is often used to attack with knee strikes in Muay Thai and MMA fights. If you are in this clinch then your opponent can pull your head down while thrusting up with his knee in the opposite direction.

CHAPTER FOUR

Hand and Elbow Strikes

This chapter looks at the main type of attacks that can be made using your hands and elbows. These are commonly used in karate, kung fu, boxing, and Muay Thai. The most obvious attack is of course a punch. However, there are many different types of punches and using correct technique can make the difference between hurting your opponent and hurting yourself. Punches are useful attacks only when your opponent is at arm's length. If your opponent is further away, then you would need to consider kicks. If they are closer, then you will need to look at closer range attacks, for example using your elbows or your knees.

Using the fist to strike, as you do when punching, can cause damage to the delicate bones in your hand. There are alternative methods of using your hands in attacks by using either the side of your hand, knife hand strike, or the back of your hand, as in back fist strike. Finally, your elbow can also be used for striking. The elbow strike can be used in both horizontal and vertical motions. This type of attack is very effective at close range and you are generally less likely to damage your elbow than your hand when using it for striking.

When training in these techniques you may find that you are able to perform stronger attacks on one side than the other. You should use your training practice to try to build upon your weaker side, to ensure that you can apply effective strikes from both sides of your body.

SUMMARY OF HAND AND ELBOW STRIKES

Stepping punch	A linear punch used to rapidly close in on your opponent
Jabbing punch	A fast, linear punch made with your leading hand
Hook-punch	A circular punch
Cross-punch	A powerful, linear punch made with your rear hand
Uppercut	A vertical punch, moving upwards towards the body or the chin
Superman-punch	A punch that is fired at the same time as you pull your knee back after a feint
Palm-strike	A strike particularly popular for self-defense
Knife hand-strike	A strike to the neck, side of head or arm using the edge of your hand
Reverse knife hand-strike	A strike to the neck or arm using the edge of your hand that can also be used as a parry
Back fist strike	A strike that whose contact point is the knuckles on your index finger and your middle finger
Horizontal elbow strike	A powerful circular attack using the elbow
Reverse horizontal elbow strike	An attack that hits with the point of the elbow
Uppercut elbow strike	An elbow attack that moves upwards and hits under the chin or body
Downward elbow strike	A dangerous finishing move to the head, collar bone, or back

Punches

In the striking arts, punches are by far the most common upper body technique. Punches are often used by untrained fighters and are the simplest of techniques to learn. All striking arts practice punching and Western boxing is based entirely around punching. Practicing individual punches is the first step to reaching the full potential of punching, but it cannot be realized until you practice using them in combinations that chain punches together. The most common targets for punches are the head and then the torso. There are many vulnerable targets in these areas and punches can be strong, swift techniques that can attack them specifically.

MAKING A FIST

It is important to understand how to correctly make a fist before punching. If you use bad technique while punching it is likely to cause you injury. Most martial arts teach punches by practicing in the air. Once the basics have been mastered, you can then move on to practicing against a punching bag. When you train with a punching bag, it will be much more obvious if there is a problem with your technique, for example, if you are bending your wrist or not closing your fist properly. This weakness will make your actions weaker and also increase the risk of injuring yourself.

When you punch, ensure that you keep your wrist straight. Your contact point should be the knuckles of your index finger and your middle finger.

In some ways, the human hand is badly suited for striking because it contains many bones and joints that are relatively delicate. Many martial arts require that fighters wear protective equipment that offers protection for their hands. Some martial artists engage in conditioning exercises, for example plunging their hands into hot sand or punching wooden targets, in an attempt to toughen their fists. Other martial artists consider exposing their hands to this kind of trauma to be more damaging than beneficial. A weak fist or wrist can result in injury when punching. For example, if your thumb sticks out then it can inadvertently get caught and damage your thumb joint.

One way to avoid injuring your fist when punching without the need for conditioning or protective equipment is to aim for soft targets, so accurate punching is an important skill. Another option is to use a palm strike.

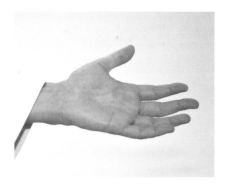

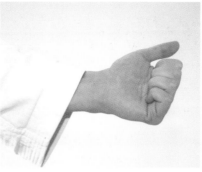

Step 1 *Hold out your hand in front of you, with your hand open and your palm facing upwards.*

Step 2 *Close your four fingers tightly by rolling them in.*

Step 3 *Pull your thumb in on top of your fingers.*

STEPPING PUNCH

Use the stepping punch to rapidly close in on an opponent. This can be useful in placing pressure on an opponent or pursuing a retreating opponent. This technique is often used in quick succession as a way of charging your opponent or pushing them out of the competition area. This is a popular attack in karate where it is called a pursuit punch, *oi-zuki*.

Step 1 *Stand in fighting stance with your left leg forward.*

Step 2 *Step forward with your right foot, landing in a long stance with your rear leg extended and your right knee bent. As you do this, push your right shoulder forward and punch with your right hand.*

Step 3 *When your arm reaches full extension, immediately pull your right shoulder back and retract your punching hand, returning to your guard position. At the same time, drag your trailing left foot in so that you return to a fighting stance.*

JABBING PUNCH

A jab is a fast, straight punch thrown from the front hand. What this punch lacks in power, it makes up for in speed. Because the jab requires relatively little effort to execute and carries a low risk of counter attack, you can use it to test an opponent's defenses or gauge distance to an opponent. It is also commonly used as a feint to open your opponent's guard. This is a popular attack in karate where it is called *kizami-zuki*. You can use a jab as an attacking move by using it simultaneously with a forward motion, often as an opening technique in an attacking combination.

Step 1 *Stand in fighting stance with your left leg forward.*

Step 2 *Slide your left leg forward and at the same time punch by pushing your left shoulder forward and extending your left arm.*

Step 3 *Pull your left shoulder back and retract your hand to the guard position. At the same time, draw your rear foot forward, resetting back to a short stance.*

You can also use the jabbing punch as a defensive technique, quickly counter striking an attacker and using the speed of an oncoming opponent to overcome any lack of power in the jab. This technique also makes use of coming off the line of the attack.

Step 1 *Face your opponent in fighting stance with your left leg forward.*

Step 2 *As your opponent launches towards you with a punch, move your right leg around behind you so that you pivot clockwise. At the same time, extend your left arm forward, aiming a left jab at your opponent's head.*

HOOK PUNCH

The hook punch uses a circular motion to land a powerful knockout blow. It is also a key punch in full contact striking arts such as boxing and Muay Thai.

A larger and more powerful version of the hook involves straightening the arm as you bring it back and then swinging in a wide circular arc at the target. This type of punch is called a "haymaker" or a "sucker punch" and, while more powerful than a hook, it is so wild and easily countered that it is rarely used by experienced fighters unless against an already stunned opponent who is unlikely to exploit this weakness.

Step 1 *Stand in fighting stance with your left leg forward.*

Step 2 *Rotate your hips anticlockwise and lift your left elbow back slightly and out to the left.*

Step 3 *Rotate your hips clockwise and punch by swinging your fist in front of you.*

Step 4 *Pull your left hand back into the guard position.*

CROSS PUNCH

A cross punch, also known as a "straight," is a straight punch thrown from the rear hand. It is a powerful punch because it uses a big rotation of the body and throws the body weight forward, but for the same reasons it is slower than throwing a jab and is prone to counter attack. Often a fighter will use what is known as a "one-two," leading with a jabbing punch and then following up with a cross punch. In karate it is called a reverse punch, *gyaku-zuki*.

Step 1 *Stand in fighting stance with your left leg forward.*

Step 2 *Slide your left leg forward and at the same time punch by straightening your right leg, pushing your right hip and shoulder forward and extending your right arm.*

Step 3 *Pull your right shoulder back and retract your hand to the guard position. At the same time, draw your rear foot forward, resetting back to a short stance.*

Pulling back the opposite hand when punching is a training mechanism used by karate practitioners that can help you to learn how to use your body correctly when punching and also to use the retracting hand to unbalance your opponent.

Step 1

Face your opponent in fighting stance with your left leg forward.

Step 2

As your opponent punches to your head with a right hook, lift your left arm to block the punch.

Step 3

Grab your opponent's right wrist.

Step 4

Pull your opponent in, by retracting your left hand, while at the same time pushing your right hip forward and punching with a right cross.

UPPERCUT

The uppercut punch is a powerful attack that travels from below its target before lifting up and hitting either the head, or if your opponent is hunched over, the body. The uppercut gets some of its power from your biceps but can also make use of your legs to get under your opponent and then lift up. This is a popular technique in boxing and Muay Thai.

Step 1 *Stand in fighting stance with your left leg forward.*

Step 2 *Bend your knees and drop your right hand slightly, but keep your right elbow bent.*

Step 3 *Straighten your legs while pushing your right hip forward and punch by lifting your right fist.*

A common combination involves using an uppercut to lift an opponent's chin, leaving them open to a follow up with a hook, potentially scoring a knockout blow.

Step 1
Face your opponent in fighting stance with your left leg forward.

Step 2
As your opponent punches with a right hook, slip slightly to the right and block with your left hand.

Step 3
Using your right hand, throw an uppercut to your opponent's chin. As you do this, bring your left hand slightly back and lift your left elbow.

Step 4
Using your left hand, throw a left hook at your opponent's head.

SUPERMAN PUNCH

This punching technique comes from the world of Thai boxing, and has become quite popular on the MMA scene. The superman punch works by using a fake knee strike to draw your opponent's guard down, creating an opening for the head level punch.

Step 1 *Stand in fighting stance with your left leg forward.*

Step 2 *Lift your right knee, shooting it towards your opponent, while drawing back your right fist ready to punch.*

Step 3 *As you drop your right knee, hop forward and begin punching with your right hand.*

Step 4 *Thrust your right leg back again but keep your weight moving forward while punching with a right cross.*

The superman punch is a bit of an all or nothing attack. If your opponent realizes what you are doing, then they can easily counter attack, but if it works then it is a very powerful attack. Before using this attack, you should lay the groundwork to give it the best chance of success. Throw some low or medium level kicking attacks so that when you begin the superman punch, your opponent will be more likely to react to the knee lift thinking it is a kick, thus creating the opening that you need.

Step 1 *Face your opponent in fighting stance.*

Step 2 *Throw a low kick at your opponent's leg. You can repeat this step as you see fit in order to program a response in your opponent.*

Step 3 *Return again to fighting stance. Your opponent is now "programmed" to expect a kick.*

Step 4 *Feint a kick by lifting your knee.*

Step 5 *As your opponent drops his guard, launch a superman punch to the head.*

PUNCHING COMBINATIONS

A common mistake by inexperienced fighters is to throw punches in isolation. This rarely represents much of a threat to an opponent because a single punch is easily blocked or evaded and can allow an opponent the opportunity to counter attack. A series of punches thrown in combination puts an opponent under more pressure and each punch can create an opening for the subsequent punch.

You can enhance your punching combination, for example, with a strong forward motion, putting your opponent firmly into defensive mode.

Step 1 *Stand in fighting stance with your left leg forward.*

Step 2 *Throw a left jab punch.*

Step 3 *Throw a right cross punch.*

Step 4 *Throw a left hook punch.*

Step 5 *Throw a right uppercut.*

Other Hand Strikes

There are of course other parts of the hand that can be used to strike with other than your fist. Using the edge of your hand, the knuckles in a back fist strike or even the fingers or finger joints. The most common of these techniques are presented here.

PALM STRIKE

A palm strike (also known as a palm heel strike) is a hand technique that hits with the base of the palm. When punching with a closed fist there is a risk of injuring your own knuckles if you happen to hit something hard and bony. The palm strike does not suffer from this problem but still has a similar hitting power to using a closed fist. A palm strike is also less likely to cause cuts than an ungloved punch and so some competitions, for example the MMA event called Pancrase, have banned punches to the head in favor of palm strikes. It is the base of the palm that is the key contact point in this attack.

When hitting with a palm strike, bend your wrist back and pull your fingers back so that you can strike with the base of your palm.

This attack can also be used in a horizontal motion, for example, attacking the floating ribs. However, it is usually aimed at the head and, in self-defense applications, it is targeted in particular at the nose or under the chin so that the opponent's head is pushed back, allowing for follow up attacks.

Step 1 *Face your opponent in fighting stance with your left leg forward.*

Step 2 *As your opponent attacks with a right hook, block with your left arm.*

Step 3 *Strike with a palm strike under your opponent's chin, lifting his head and leaving him exposed to subsequent attacks.*

KNIFE HAND STRIKE

The knife hand strike is sometimes called the sword hand strike. This is the strike that has become popularly known as the "karate chop." In karate, it is known as *shuto uchi*.

The knife hand strike hits with the fleshy edge of the hand

Step 1 *Stand in fighting stance with your left leg forward.*

Step 2 *Open your right hand, keeping your fingers and thumb firmly together. Lift your right elbow and pull it back so that your right hand finishes to the side of your right ear with your palm facing out away from you.*

Step 3 *Rotate your right hip forwards, and extend your right arm forward so that your right hand moves in an arc towards your target, striking with the fleshy edge of your hand.*

A knife hand strike can be used to strike the side of your opponent's head, with the strike moving horizontally. This strike can also be used to strike the neck, moving diagonally downwards. Since this technique is regarded as too dangerous to be allowed in competitions, it is hard to come by real life accounts of the effect of this strike. However, on the BBC television program "The Indestructibles," a British martial artist, Terry Wingrove, demonstrated how he could knockout an opponent with a single knife hand strike to the neck. Obviously, when practicing this technique with a sparring partner, you should not attempt to reproduce this result, and so extra care should be taken to stop your strikes short of your target.

Step 1 *Face your opponent in fighting stance with your left leg forward.*

Step 2 *As your opponent attacks with a right hook, block with your left arm and prepare to strike by lifting your right hand up alongside your head.*

Step 3 *Strike with a knife hand strike to the side of your opponent's neck.*

REVERSE KNIFE HAND STRIKE

In karate, this technique is often used to parry attacks and is referred to as *shuto uke*.

Step 1 *Stand in fighting stance with your left leg forward.*

Step 2 *Open your hands. Push your right hand across to the left side of your body while bringing your left hand across to the right side of your head so that your left palm faces towards your right ear.*

Step 3 *Pull your right hand back to the middle of your body, while pushing your left arm back over to the left. As you do this, rotate your forearm so that the fleshy part of your hand points outward and you strike using the outside edge of your hand.*

This technique is most commonly targeted at the forearm or the neck.

Step 1 *Face your opponent in fighting stance with your left leg forward.*

Step 2 *As your opponent attacks with a right cross, step off the line of the attack by moving your right foot to the right and parry the attack with your right hand while preparing for a reverse knife hand strike with your left hand.*

Step 3 *Strike your opponent's forearm with a reverse knife hand strike using your left hand.*

Step 4 *Grab hold of your opponent's right forearm using your left hand, while preparing for a reverse knife hand strike with your right hand.*

Step 5 *Step forward with your right leg and strike to side of your opponent's neck with a reverse knife hand strike using your right hand.*

BACK FIST STRIKE

The back fist strike is most commonly used in kung fu, usually as part of a chain of hand strikes. It is also used in karate and is called *uraken uchi*.

It is important to hit with the knuckles of your index finger and your middle finger, rather than the delicate bones in the back of your hand. To do this you should ensure that you rotate your forearm so that these big knuckles are nearest to the target. You should also allow your wrist to flex, so that your knuckles flick towards your target.

Step 1 *Stand in fighting stance with your left leg forward.*

Step 2 *Lift your left elbow and bring your left fist alongside your right ear.*

Step 3 *Swing your left arm around in an arc and straighten your arm so that your fist whips forward. Take due care to not hyperextend your elbow joint during this motion.*

Elbow Strikes

Elbow strikes are effective short-range attacks that can be used in the grappling phase of combat. The elbow is a particularly bony and tough part of the body and so can be used for heavy strikes against a great many target areas. Elbow strikes tend to cause your opponent cuts, especially when you hit the face, so many martial arts forbid the use of elbows in competitions. In contests where they are allowed, for example MMA and Muay Thai fights, they are often used specifically because they can give cuts which can bring a fight to an end with a technical knockout (TKO).

HORIZONTAL ELBOW STRIKE

In Muay Thai, the horizontal elbow strike is called *sok tad*. In karate, it is called a circular elbow strike, *mawashi empi uchi*. This powerful attack is usually aimed at the head but can also be used as a body blow. It can be used during the grappling phase of combat as well as during ground fighting.

Step 1 *Stand in fighting stance with your left leg forward.*

Step 2 *Lift your right elbow back to the side of your body.*

Step 3 *Push your right hip forward so that your body rotates anticlockwise. Throw your elbow forward in a circular motion.*

If you try using a horizontal elbow strike when your opponent is in the punching range, it is more than likely to be easily blocked. Even so, there is a chance that it may still be effective, because the elbow strike is powerful and a weak block may well collapse. However, this elbow strike is best used when already at close range during the grappling phase of combat.

Step 1 *Stand holding your opponent in a clinch, with your left arm over your opponent's neck.*

Step 2 *When your opponent lifts his head, lift your right elbow.*

Step 3 *Throw a horizontal elbow strike at his head using your right elbow.*

In Muay Thai, a common variation of the horizontal elbow strike is the slashing elbow, *sok ti*. This is performed in the same way as the horizontal elbow but, instead of travelling parallel to the ground, the elbow starts high up and then slashes diagonally down and across.

REVERSE HORIZONTAL ELBOW STRIKE

In Muay Thai, the reverse horizontal elbow is called *sok klab*. In karate, it is called a side elbow strike, *yoko empi uchi*.

Step 1 *Stand in fighting stance with your left leg forward.*

Step 2 *Slide your left foot back and rotate your body clockwise so that your chest faces to the side. At the same time, bring your left arm back so that your left fist travels to your right shoulder and your left elbow lifts and points out away from you.*

Step 3 *Slide your left foot forward while jabbing your left elbow forward.*

You can use the reverse horizontal elbow in combination with the horizontal elbow strike during the grappling phase of combat.

Step 1 *Stand holding your opponent in a clinch, with your right arm over your opponent's neck.*

Step 2 *When your opponent lifts his head, throw a horizontal elbow strike at his head using your left elbow.*

Step 3 *Continue moving your elbow through and past your opponent, turning your body to the right.*

Step 4 *Move your body weight back into your opponent while throwing the same elbow back at your opponent's head so that you hit with a reverse horizontal elbow strike.*

UPPERCUT ELBOW

In Muay Thai, the uppercut elbow strike is called *sok kun*. In karate, it is called a rising elbow strike, *age empi uchi*. It is a close range attack that can be used in the grappling phase of combat.

Step 1 *Stand in fighting stance with your left leg forward.*

Step 2 *Push your right elbow forward so that it starts to lift in front of you and your right hand moves towards your right shoulder.*

Step 3 *Push your right hip forward and keep moving your elbow up in front of you so that your right hand finishes next to your right ear. Your elbow should be targeting your opponent's chin.*

In karate, a closed fist is a common technique, but in Muay Thai it is usually done with an open hand, mainly because the big gloves worn in sparring would get in the way as your hand passes your head and opening the hand avoids this.

The uppercut elbow can be used as a bold counter striking technique that involves driving forward into your opponent.

Step 1 *Face your opponent in fighting stance with your left leg forward.*

Step 2 *As your opponent throws a right hook, block the attack with your left arm.*

Step 3 *Grab your opponent's right arm and pull with your left arm, while stepping forward with your right foot. Throw an uppercut elbow at your opponent's chin.*

DOWNWARD ELBOW STRIKE

Also known as the "straight 12-6" dropping elbow or spiking downward elbow. This technique strikes with the point of the elbow in a downward direction. Possible targets include the top of the head, the nose, the clavicle (collar bone) or the spine, depending on the position of your opponent at the time. It is important to note that the spine is a very dangerous target to strike and should only be considered a possibility in a life or death self-defense situation. Consequently, this sort of attack tends to be banned in competitions.

Step 1 *Stand in fighting stance with your left leg forward.*

Step 2 *Step forward with your right foot and lift your right arm.*

Step 3 *Drop your right elbow, rotating your forearm so that the palm of your hand faces in towards you. You can increase the power of the technique by dropping your body weight into the strike.*

One use of this technique is to attack an opponent attempting to shoot in take you down by grabbing your legs. When practicing this with a sparring partner, be sure to stop the elbow strike short of your opponent so as to avoid an injury.

Step 1 *Face your opponent in fighting stance with your left leg forward.*

Step 2 *As your opponent shoots in, straighten your right arm lifting your right fist above your head.*

Step 3 *Strike your opponent's back by dropping your elbow.*

*Of old the expert in battle would first
make himself invincible and then wait for
his enemy to expose his vulnerability.*

~ Sun Tzu

CHAPTER FIVE

Defenses

Having looked at a number of different strikes that can be made against you using the hands and elbows in the previous chapter, we now turn to a few different approaches to defending yourself. The most natural thing to do when defending yourself is to throw your arms out around your head to protect it. Training yourself in defense techniques will help you to develop a more controlled response that can be used to then launch a counter attack.

Blocking is probably the first thing that comes to mind when thinking about defenses. This is actually the last type of defense that you would actually want to use, as it is the one that is most likely, after the attack that is, to hurt you. There are subtler approaches to defense that you can use that may avert any contact at all with your opponent. This takes the form of slipping and ducking the attack. These techniques use the action of moving your body out of harm's way as the defense. You will still often get the arms into a position to enable you to either parry or block in case your attempt to slip or duck has been unsuccessful.

Parrying and blocking are then the more direct responses to an attack. Blocking is to put a dead stop on the attack, whereas parrying just changes the direction of the attack away from you. Once you have mastered the techniques for these defenses, it is useful to practice these with a partner. This will give you a better understanding of distancing and effectiveness of your defense than if you just trained alone.

SUMMARY OF DEFENSES	
Slip	Avoiding a straight attack by moving off to the side
Duck	Avoiding a head level attack by going under it
Parry	Deflecting a straight attack
Block	Stopping an attack by putting an arm or a knee in the way
High-level block	Defending against attacks aimed at your head
Middle level block	Defending against attacks aimed at your body
Low level block	Defending against low level attacks
Two-handed block	Stopping powerful circular attacks
Cross block	Stopping downward swinging attacks

SLIP

Slipping is a way of avoiding a straight attack, usually aimed at the head, by moving the whole body out of the way, off to the side. This does not need to be a big movement, just enough to get clear of the attack so that you can slip past it. Slipping is a very valuable technique because it allows you to avoid an attack while leaving both of your hands free.

When slipping, it is important not to move into a position that sets up your opponent's next attack. For example, if you slip a jab you should be wary of moving towards your opponent's cross, because jabs are often intended to set you up to do just that. So if your opponent jabs with a left, then you should move to your right, away from any potential follow up right cross. This is called a slip to the outside.

Step 1 *Face your opponent in fighting stance with your left leg forward.*

Step 2 *As your opponent throws a left jab, step out to the right with your right foot so that your head moves slightly to the right, avoiding the punch.*

Step 3 *Immediately, punch to the head with a right cross.*

DUCK

Ducking, sometimes called bobbing, is like slipping but instead of moving sideways, you drop down under an attack. It can work against both straight attacks, like a jab or a cross, and against circular attacks like a hook. When ducking, you need to keep your hands up near your head so that you can still block if you time the duck incorrectly. Having your elbows protecting your body and chin will also help to protect you in case something goes wrong and you end up ducking into a knee attack. You also need to make sure that you use your knees to duck rather than bending too much at your waist, so that you can keep an eye on your opponent while you duck and keep your head in a safer position. In boxing, it is more common to bend from the waist mainly because there is no risk of a knee strike in that sport.

Step 1

Face your opponent in fighting stance with your left leg forward.

Step 2

As your opponent throws a right hook, move your head slightly to your right, away from the punch. As you do this, bend your knees so that you duck down out of the path of your opponent's hook.

Step 3

Stay low and roll to your left so that you move under the punch and counter with a right cross.

Step 4

Straighten your knees and follow up with a left hook.

BLOCK AND PARRY

If someone throws a strike at you, be it a punch, a kick, or an elbow, the best way to avoid getting hurt is to get out of the way. Sometimes it just isn't possible to get out of the way of an attack and so you need to use a block or a parry to reduce the damage that the attack will do. A block is a technique that stops an attack dead by getting in the way of it. A parry is subtler in that rather than facing the force of the attack head on, it deflects the attack, redirecting it so that it passes by harmlessly. Blocks are most useful against circular attacks and parries are most useful against straight attacks. If it is a powerful attack, such as an elbow strike, a hook, or a roundhouse kick then this might still hurt you but it is far better to take a big hit on somewhere like your forearm than on your face.

A block can do more than just thwart an attack. A powerful block can be more like an attack to an opponent's arm or leg, and in a self-defense situation this could leave an attacker thinking twice about throwing another punch. A strong parry can redirect an attack in such a way that it can unbalance an attacker leaving them open to a counter attack.

Usually blocks are done with the forearm or the hands, but it is also possible to block using other tough parts of your body such as the shoulders, elbows or knees. Parries can also be done with the forearm but are commonly done using an open hand.

HIGH LEVEL DEFENSE

Use this technique to block a downward or sideways swinging attack at your head. It can also be used as a parry to deflect straight attacks aimed at your head. In karate, this technique is called a rising block, *age uke*.

Step 1 *Face your opponent in fighting stance with your left leg forward.*

Step 2 *Lift your left fist so that your forearm goes in front of your face.*

Step 3 *Rotate your forearm so that your elbow lifts and the back of your fist faces towards you.*

This high block works well when combined with a ducking movement, with your body dropping down while the block sends an attack up over your head.

Step 1 *Face your opponent in fighting stance with your left leg forward.*

Step 2 *As your opponent attacks with a stepping punch aimed at your head, drop your weight while deflecting the punch over your head using your left forearm.*

Step 3 *Counter punch using a right cross.*

You can increase the effectiveness of this counter attack by reducing the time between the block and the punch. This is especially true if your opponent is moving in towards you as he attacks because then he will be moving into your punch. The ultimate objective of this tactic is to punch at the same time as you block. In Krav Maga, this is known as bursting.

MIDDLE LEVEL DEFENSE FROM THE OUTSIDE

An outside block, called *soto uke* in karate, can actually be used to parry as well as block and can be used to deflect an attack to the side. Rather confusingly, this block is sometimes referred to as an inside block. To understand this, you need to consider your view when you are fighting. The center of your view is considered the inside and the edges of your view, to the left and right, are considered to be outside. The people who call this technique outside block do so because it approaches from the outside. Those who call it inside block do so because it moves towards the inside.

Step 1 *Stand in fighting stance with your left leg forward.*

Step 2 *Bring your left arm out to the left. As you do this, rotate your forearm so that the back of your fist faces towards you.*

Step 3 *Swing your arm back across to the right. As you do this, rotate your forearm so that the back of your fist faces away from you.*

This technique is useful for parrying attacks that are travelling straight into your center, for example, against a stepping punch aimed at your body.

Step 1 *Face your opponent in fighting stance with your left leg forward.*

Step 2 *As your opponent steps forward and punches, pivot clockwise by moving your right foot round behind you to the left and deflect the punch using an outside block.*

Step 3 *Counter attack with a right cross.*

MIDDLE LEVEL DEFENSE FROM THE INSIDE

An inside block, called *uchi uke* in karate, can be used to block an attack to the side in the opposite direction to an outside block. Again, rather confusingly, this block is sometimes referred to as an outside block. The people who call this technique inside block do so because it approaches from the inside. Those who call it outside block do so because it moves towards the outside.

Step 1 *Stand in fighting stance with your left leg forward.*

Step 2 *Bring your left hand down to your right side with the back of your fist facing towards you.*

Step 3 *Swing your arm back across to the left. As you do this, rotate your forearm so that the back of your fist faces away from you.*

This technique is useful for defending against an attack that is travelling around to hit you from the side, for example, a hooking punch or roundhouse kick.

Step 1 *Face your opponent in fighting stance with your left leg forward.*

Step 2 *As your opponent throws a right hook, pivot counterclockwise by moving your right foot out to the right and stop the attack using an inside block.*

LOW LEVEL DEFENSE

In karate, this block is called a low-level sweep, *gedan barai*. This technique is most useful when used as a parry to deflect low punches and kicks.

Step 1 *Stand in fighting stance with your left leg forward.*

Step 2 *Bring your left fist over to the right.*

Step 3 *Swing down with your left hand so that it finishes just above your left knee.*

This low level block can be used to parry a front kick. It is important to parry this type of attack rather than block it because an opponent's leg is likely to be stronger than your forearm so a head on collision is likely to injure you. It is better to move out the way of the kick and use your arm to deflect it in the opposite direction. Because of the circular motion of the low level block, it is possible to get your arm underneath your opponent's leg allowing you to unbalance them.

Step 1 *Face your opponent in fighting stance with your left leg forward.*

Step 2 *As your opponent launches a front kick at you, move off the line of the attack by moving your right foot to the right. Use a low level block with your left arm to deflect the kick to the side.*

Step 3 *Continue the circular motion of your left arm so that you hook it under your opponent's kicking leg while shifting your left leg in slightly so that you slide in close to your opponent. Grab hold of your opponent's jacket with your right hand and step forward with your right foot and lift it behind your opponent's left leg.*

Step 4 *Push your opponent back with your left arm while lifting their right leg with your left arm. Pull your right leg into the back of your opponent's left leg.*

Step 5 *Reap your opponent's leg with your right leg so that they are taken down to the ground.*

TWO-HANDED DEFENSE

If you are trying to block a really powerful attack such as a hook, a roundhouse kick, or a horizontal elbow strike, sometimes it can be worth using both arms to stop the attack. Using one arm could mean that a strong attack could collapse the defending arm and you could end up with your own fist hitting you in the face. Using two arms pretty much doubles your stopping power. The main drawback of this is that using both arms to block makes it harder for you to counter attack and can leave you open to a follow up attack.

Step 1 *Face your opponent in fighting stance with your left leg forward.*

Step 2 *As your opponent strikes with a left horizontal elbow strike, bring both your arms out to your right side, blocking the attack.*

TWO-HANDED CROSS DEFENSE

A cross block, called *juji uke* in karate, is a type of two handed block that can be used to stop an attack that swings down. It can also be used as a parry to deflect straight attacks aimed at the head.

Step 1 *Stand in fighting stance with your left leg forward.*

Step 2 *Open both of your hands and bring your left arm up and across to the right. At the same time, lift your right arm up and across to the left so that your right forearm crosses your left forearm.*

Step 3 *Keep lifting your arms so that the "cross" moves above your head.*

Like all two-handed blocks, this technique's main drawback is that it commits both of your hands, leaving you prone to any follow-up attacks. It therefore should only be used when a dangerous attack absolutely must be stopped. One example would be a stabbing attack with a knife because in this situation the knife represents a serious threat, so it makes more sense to commit everything to stop it.

Step 1 *Face your opponent in fighting stance with your left leg forward.*

Step 2 *As your opponent strikes down with a stabbing motion, lift both arms and block with a cross block.*

Step 3 *By bringing your left hand onto your opponent's elbow and grabbing his wrist with your right hand, apply an arm bar.*

I fear not the man who has practiced 10,000 kicks once,
but I fear the man who has practiced one kick 10,000 times.

~ Bruce Lee

CHAPTER SIX

Foot and Knee Strikes

Some martial arts consider kicks to be the best form of attack because the legs contain the biggest muscles in the body and produces the most powerful strike. Another advantage is that using your legs leaves your hands free for defense. Kicks can also have a superior range compared with a punch. Some martial arts put a low priority on kicks either because they can result in a loss of stability or because kicks are not allowed in their competitions.

The strikes shown in this chapter are common in taekwondo, karate, kung fu, and Muay Thai. The front kick and the knee strike are the easiest to master as they mostly use actions found in normal everyday activities. All the other kicks are more difficult, either because they require rotation or because they use a hip action that you may not be used to or that your flexibility does not allow.

Both leg strength and flexibility will make your kicks more powerful. If, like in taekwondo, you wish to master the flashy high kicks, then you should work on your flexibility too. Kicking beyond your comfortable range of motion will increase the risk of injury. The stretching chapter later in this book, looks at a variety of stretches that you can incorporate into your training. Remember that mastering the most advanced kicks and increasing your flexibility take times.

Once you have mastered the technique with these kicks you can think about introducing some targeting exercises by using a strike shield. This can help you to ensure that your kick is both travelling in the right direction and that it is making contact with your intended target.

SUMMARY OF KICKS	
Front kick	Fast, straight, easy to use attack
Roundhouse kick	Powerful circular attack
Side kick	Slow but powerful straight attack
Back kick	Powerful straight attack
Spinning hook kick	Circular attack
Tornado kick	Advanced circular attack
Knee strike	Powerful close range attack
Flying knee strike	A launched knee strike, giving it greater range
Curve knee strike	A short range attack using the knee in a circular motion

FRONT KICK

The front kick is the easiest kick to master and can be used as a defensive stopping attack, as a stealthy and quick self-defense kick or as a flashy head level kick. In taekwondo, it is called *ap chagi*, in karate, this kick is called *mae geri* and in Muay Thai it is called *teh trong*.

When using a front kick, you should hit with the ball of your foot. To do this, point your foot at the target and pull your toes back.

The front kick has many potential target areas, for example, the body, the shins, the groin and, of course, the head. A low front kick is less likely to be caught by a defensive maneuver from your opponent than a higher kick.

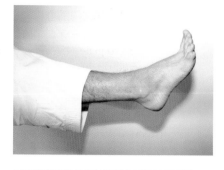

Step 1 *Stand in fighting stance with your left leg forward.*

Step 2 *Lift your right knee, keeping your knee bent.*

Step 3 *Kick by extending your right leg, while pushing forward with your hips.*

Step 4 *Retract your right foot back by bending your knee.*

Step 5 *Step forward with your right foot so that you return to a fighting stance.*

ROUNDHOUSE KICK

In taekwondo, this kick is called *dolryo chagi*, in karate, it is called a circular kick, *mawashi geri* and in Muay Thai it is known as *Teh Tud*. It is probably the most popular of all the kicks in martial arts contests that allow them. It uses a big hip rotation to generate power and this action can make the roundhouse kick difficult to learn. However, once you have mastered the hip action, it becomes a fast and powerful technique. A clean hit to the head will often cause a knockout, making this kick popular in fighting contests where this is the main objective, for example kickboxing and MMA contests. The ability to throw a roundhouse kick to the head takes on particular importance in kyokushin-kai karate, and WTF taekwondo contests where head punches are not permitted but head kicks are allowed.

There are three contact areas that are commonly used with this kick.

Area 1 *The instep is often used as the attacking area during training and friendly sparring in martial arts like karate and taekwondo. This gives more of a slapping action to this kick.*

Area 2 *The ball of the foot hits with a more focused impact and can be dangerous if aimed at the floating ribs.*

Area 3 *Hitting with the shin is common in Muay Thai. It relies more on power than on accuracy and can be used effectively against the body and thighs. This method of kicking represents the best way to hit hard without having to worry about injuring your foot.*

The roundhouse kick is useful when targeted at the body, particularly against opponents with a strong high guard. A low roundhouse kick aimed at the legs is often used in Thai boxing and MMA fights as a way to reduce an opponent's mobility. In contests where attacks directed at the legs are not allowed, it is often still possible to sweep the legs using a motion very similar to a low level roundhouse kick.

Step 1 *Stand in fighting stance with your left leg forward.*

Step 2 *Lift your right knee to the side of your body.*

Step 3 *Rotate your right hip in towards your opponent. At the same time, rotate your left foot so that your toes point out to the left.*

Step 4 *Extend your leg so that your leg swings in and kicks your opponent.*

Step 5 *Retract your right foot.*

Step 6 *Step down into a fighting stance with your right foot forward.*

If your opponent has a strong guard, then an isolated roundhouse kick to the middle level is likely to be blocked. It is therefore important that this kick is not used in isolation. By using high level attacks, you can draw your opponent's guard up, creating an opening for a roundhouse kick.

Step 1 *Face your opponent in fighting stance with your left leg forward.*

Step 2 *As your opponent throws a left jab at your head, slip to the right.*

Step 3 *Immediately throw a right cross at your opponent's head.*

Step 4 *Immediately follow up with a roundhouse kick using your right leg, aimed at your opponent's body.*

SIDE KICK

This is an impressive looking kick that requires leg strength, flexibility, and balance to perform correctly. There are two distinct ways to use this side kick. One way is to thrust the kick, pushing through to full extension. This type of kick is good for pushing an opponent back or stopping an oncoming opponent. The other way is to snap the kick back, shooting the kick in and then once the impact has occurred, to pull it back out again. Doing the kick this way reduces the chance of an opponent catching your leg while also allowing you to quickly follow up with another attack. In taekwondo, this kick is called *yop chagi* and in karate it is known as *yoko geri*. This kick requires a big hip rotation and side flexibility. It is not uncommon it to take students many years of practice to master it.

Your contact area for this kick is your heel. Your toes should be pulled in and your foot should be slightly angled down.

Step 1 *Stand in fighting stance with your left leg forward.*

Step 2 *Lift your right knee and rotate your body around to the left so that your right knee is brought over to the left. As you do this, you should switch your guard around so that your right arm is up in front of you.*

Step 3 *Lift your right hip and angle your right leg so that the base of your foot aims in the direction you want to kick. You should allow your supporting leg to pivot on the toe so that your left heel moves towards the direction you are going to kick.*

Step 4 *Kick by extending your right leg. The higher you kick, the more your upper body will have to angle away from the kick, but avoid leaning away from the kick any more than you need to. Keep your guard up and look in the direction you are kicking.*

Step 5 *Retract your right leg.*

Step 6 *Step forward, returning to a fighting stance.*

While this kick looks impressive when thrown to the body or head level, it is not as practical as a low level kick in self-defense situations. A more realistic application of the side kick is as a low level kick aimed at an opponent's knee. You can practice this with a sparring partner, preferably at a safe slow speed so as to avoid damaging the knee.

Step 1 *Your opponent grabs your right wrist with his right hand.*

Step 2 *Trap your opponent's hand with your left hand and use a circular movement to apply a wrist lock, pressing the edge of your right hand into the your opponent's wrist joint.*

Step 3 *Lift your right foot so that it is higher than your opponent's knee and bring it over to the left.*

Step 4 *Push your leg down into the side of your opponent's right knee. SAFETY TIP: Do this technique slowly, so as to avoid injuring your sparring partner. If you are being kicked in the knee, you need to allow your knee to move with the kick rather than trying to resist it.*

Step 5 *Your kick should turn your opponent to his left. As you step down, keep hold of your opponent with your right hand and throw a left cross at his head.*

BACK KICK

Kick boxers call this the turn back kick or just turn kick. In taekwondo, this kick is called *dwi chagi* and in karate it is called back kick, *ushiro geri*. It uses a strong thrusting action that is difficult to stop but because it shoots backwards, it can also be difficult to aim. The best target for this kick is at your opponent's stomach or solar plexus. Watch out for counter attacks. If your opponent sees this kick coming, then it is all too easy to side step and either punch you while you are facing the wrong way or even to get hold of your leg as this kick can be comparatively slow.

The contact area of this kick is predominantly the heel of your foot. Try to angle your foot downwards and pull your toes in.

Step 1 *Stand in fighting stance with your left leg forward.*

Step 2 *Pivot 180 degrees clockwise.*

Step 3 *Lift your right foot so that it is close to your left knee.*

Step 4 *Kick by extending your right leg behind you.*

Step 5 *Pull your right foot straight back to your left knee.*

Step 6 *Step through with your right foot.*

SPINNING HOOK KICK

This kick is most commonly seen performed by taekwon-do practitioners who call it the hook kick, *huryeo chagi*. It is also practiced in karate, where it is called a back reverse circular kick, *ushiro ura mawashi geri*. In Muay Thai, it is called a spinning heel kick, *teh glub lang*.

For friendly sparring, the safest way to contact with this kick is to use the base of your foot. In full contact fights it is more common to use the heel.

Step 1 *Stand in fighting stance with your left leg forward.*

Step 2 *Pivot on the spot, 180 degrees clockwise.*

Step 3 *Continue rotating clockwise and extend your right leg out to the side*

Step 4 *Continue rotating and swing your leg through.*

Step 5 *Once you have swung your foot through your target area, bend your knee and continue rotating so that you return to your start position.*

You can use the hook kick in combination with the roundhouse kick. For example, this would mean kicking your opponent on one side with a roundhouse kick and then hooking around to catch them also on the other side. The disadvantage of this kick is that there is a moment where you are turned away from your opponent.

TORNADO KICK

This impressive looking maneuver uses a full 360-degree rotation to build up extra rotational energy while also confusing your opponent. It is initially a difficult technique to learn and requires that you are first comfortable with how to do a roundhouse kick smoothly and quickly before adding the extra rotation. This technique is mainly seen in taekwondo contests, where a well-placed technique can land a knockout blow.

Step 1 *Stand in fighting stance with your left leg forward.*

Step 2 *Pivot on the spot, 180 degrees clockwise.*

Step 3 *Keep rotating and lift your right knee bringing it through to the front.*

Step 4 *As your left hip comes forward, put your right foot down on the ground and throw a roundhouse kick with your left leg.*

KNEE STRIKE

The knee strike is a powerful close range attack that can be used against an opponent's body. This technique is disallowed in most combat sports but is permitted in MMA and Muay Thai fights. It is also an important self-defense technique. The most commonly used knee strike is the straight knee, which involves thrusting the knee straight forward or up into the opponent's body or head. Often it is used while holding the opponent in a double collar tie, a maneuver that is called *hak kor aiyara* in Muay Thai.

Step 1 *Start holding your opponent in a clinch*

Step 2 *Pull your hips back.*

Step 3 *Pull down on the back of your opponent's head so that he moves in towards you. At the same time, thrust your hips forward and lift your knee and strike to the head or body.*

FLYING KNEE STRIKE

You can also use this technique at range by launching yourself forward. This is called the flying knee or, in Muay Thai, *Hanuman thayarn*. Although charging in with a flying knee can be a reckless move, it does overcome somewhat the limited range of the front knee strike and has a proven track record in MMA fights of getting a quick knockout when fighters have managed to connect with the head.

Step 1 *Start facing your opponent in fighting stance with your left leg forward.*

Step 2 *Lift your right knee and launch yourself towards you opponent, pushing your hips forwards for extra range. Keep your knee bent, so that your foot is still pointing back somewhat as you do this.*

CURVE KNEE STRIKE

Another way to use a knee strike is to lift your hip out to the side, so that the knee comes in from the side in a circular path, similar to a hook punch. This is called a curve knee or a side knee. It can be used at an even closer range than the front knee. The action used to perform this technique is similar to the roundhouse kick but strikes with a bent knee.

Step 1 *Start with your opponent holding you in a close clinch, such as a bear hug.*

Step 2 *Prepare by bringing your knee out to the side, cocking your hip back.*

Step 3 *Lift your right knee out to the side and rotate your hips, pushing your knee into your opponent's ribs.*

Never interrupt your enemy when he is making a mistake.
~ Napoleon Bonaparte

CHAPTER SEVEN

Break Falling

Break falling is the art of landing while minimizing how much you get hurt. This is an essential skill for a martial artist wishing to practice any throwing skills or take downs with a training partner, because without effective break falling skills, practicing these techniques in anything like a realistic manner would quickly result in injury. Break falling is also a useful everyday skill because it can be used when you fall for whatever reason.

Falling isn't the problem; it's hitting the ground that does the damage. The body's natural instinct is to put out a hand to break the fall, but this will focus all the energy of the fall into that arm and can result in a broken wrist or even a broken collarbone as the energy is transmitted up the arm to the shoulder. Break falling techniques aim to override this instinctive reaction, by training you to spread out the impact of hitting the ground. Positioning the body so that the impact occurs on a surface of the body that is as big and as flat as possible does this.

It is useful both inside and outside the martial arts training environment. In training, it can be used to recover from throws and also to get out of awkward holds. In everyday life, it can help you react effectively when you slip or fall. Break falling training, like all martial arts, is all about building up a reaction to a particular situation. You should learn to gain control over your instincts to hold out your hands as you fall and instead to prepare yourself to impact the ground with as much of the fleshy part of your body as is appropriate for that particular kind of fall.

This chapter looks at falling forwards, backwards and sideways. It also presents ways to elegantly recover from the fall by rolling through techniques. Practicing break falling should always be done in an appropriate environment with the right equipment. Otherwise, the training itself can be dangerous.

SUMMARY OF BREAK FALLS	
Front break fall	Useful for falls where you go directly forwards and don't have time to perform the front rolling break fall.
Back break fall	Useful for situations where you fall or are thrown directly onto your back.
Side break fall	The most practically useful break fall. This can help you to recover from many martial arts throws.
Front rolling break fall	Can be useful as part of a routine to get out of a lock or hold or when you are thrown forwards.

Break Falling Myths

Break falling doesn't hurt. - Of course it does. Repeatedly throwing yourself on a mat or a hard surface is bound to cause some aches and pains.

Knowing how to break fall means that I will never get hurt when falling over. – Break falling correctly should help to reduce the risk of injury, but it certainly doesn't mean that you will always walk away completely unharmed.

Break falling means I am safe. – It is fine in a controlled environment, where you have mats, the surface is even and clean. However, if you take a look around outside of this environment, it is a completely different situation. Raised surfaces, walls and objects are all examples of things you will commonly find that are likely to make break falling more dangerous.

How about falling from a height? – Break falling mostly works from ground level. The further you fall, the greater the risk.

Training tips

1. Start your break falling training using thick, supportive mats.

2. You should relax your arms and torso while performing break falls. The more you tense up, the more you are likely to hurt yourself or to perform the break fall incorrectly.

3. Your hands should be cupped.

4. Hold your head in tension away from the direction of the fall.

5. Maximize the surface area of your body that makes contact with the ground at first impact.

6. Aim to use fleshy parts of your body to break the fall, like your thighs, and not your bony parts, like your elbows or spine.

7. Slap the ground hard at the point of impact.

8. Gain control of your instinct to push your hands or elbows out to break your fall.

Martial arts like judo or jujutsu that routinely use takedowns will teach students break falling techniques at an early stage. In the striking arts, like karate or taekwondo, break falling is sometimes taught but it is usually not a core part of any training program. It's quite common for advanced students in these types of martial arts to never have had any formal training in break falling. However, break falling training is an important skill for these martial artists particularly if they take part in free fighting where trips are allowed. It is important to remember that although the striking arts emphasize strikes over throws and the scoring systems in their competitions bias against throws, usually throws are not precluded. For example, the World Karate Federation (WKF) competitions award points for successful throws (although you rarely see anyone attempt one) and traditional karate kata are positively littered with self-defense combinations designed to throw or trip an opponent (though many practitioners do not realize this).

Always practice break falling on a soft surface, for example, judo mats provide adequate cushioning for break falling. You know when you have completed a break fall successfully, as you will only hear one sound, as you impact the ground all at the same time. If you make more than one sound then you know that your technique needs more work. Break falling doesn't mean that you won't get any bruises and indeed repeated break falling may hurt afterwards. The idea is to minimize the risk of a more serious injury, like a bone fracture or break. You should always try to keep your head tucked in and your hands should be cupped as they make impact with the ground. An explanation sometimes offered is that the air captured in your hands is provides some cushioning to the fall. However, a more reasonable explanation is that it simply engages muscles in the hand and protects the smaller and more fragile bones of the fingers.

FRONT BREAK FALL

This break fall uses the forearms to absorb the impact of the fall. This technique is particularly important in judo where competitors will intentionally try to fall on their front and so avoid landing on their back, which would result in their opponent scoring a point. Ideally, you would want to roll out of this fall using the forward roll. However, there are occasions when that may not be possible and this break fall is useful for those times.

Step 1 *Start in a kneeling position with your arms bent and your forearms in front of your face. Your palms should face away from you and your hands should be cupped, ready for the break fall.*

Step 2 *Land flat on your forearms and hands. Keep your chin up away from the ground.*

BACK BREAK FALL

The ability to fall backward safely is a useful skill, both in a martial arts and a general context. Leg sweeps and slips in everyday life could leave you falling backwards. The temptation as always is to either push your hands or your elbows out underneath you. Even worse, unless you hold your head tightly to your chest during your fall, as a trained break falling student should do, you may find that because you are not tensing those muscles, your head flops back and may hit the ground with some intensity. The back break fall technique is shown here from a seated starting position. However, it is possible to use the same technique when starting from a standing position. Your aim would be to first get yourself into the seated starting position shown from standing and then to continue with the break fall as normal.

Break Fall

Step 1 *Start with your right foot on the ground and your left foot directly below your right knee. Have the left knee on the ground roughly perpendicular to your right leg. Hold your arms crossed, out in front of you. Your arms should be relaxed. Tuck your chin in to your chest and aim to maintain this head position throughout the fall and the recovery.*

Step 2 *Roll backwards and uncross your arms, with your palms facing towards the ground. Your hands should be cupped.*

Step 3 *Ensure that your left foot is in contact with the back of your right knee as you fall. At the same time your back impacts the ground, you should slap your hands onto the ground either side of you. Let your right leg rise up above you. Remember to keep your chin close to your chest throughout, so that your head does not hit the ground.*

Rolling out can be used to recover from a backward fall. Your aim is to continue using the momentum of your fall to turn you over and to right yourself back into the starting position. This aspect of break falling is emphasized in martial arts like jujutsu and aikido where exercises involve flowing with the technique. In judo and MMA, this kind of move is less common because your opponent is expected to be holding you as you fall, preventing this sort of recovery.

Recovery

Step 1 *Continuing the motion from the fall, let your right leg rise over you and in the direction of your opposite shoulder. Carry through the circular motion and let your right foot reach the ground, while turning you over.*

Step 2 *Pull yourself back into your starting position.*

SIDE BREAK FALL

If you are thrown, then chances are that you will fall on your side. This is by far the most common break fall that is needed to recover from throws in, for example, jujutsu and karate. During this exercise, you want to avoid putting too much pressure on your hips as you impact the ground. You want to impact with as wide and fleshy a surface area as possible. The temptation again will be to stick on your hand or your elbow. This must be avoided, as even if you are training on mats, this will hurt. Remember, you also want to hold your head in as firmly as possible to avoid any whiplash. The recovery from this fall uses a roll to the side.

Break Fall

Step 1 *Start in a kneeling position with your right foot and left knee on the ground. Place your right hand on your right knee. Hold your head in tension, away from the direction in which you are falling.*

Step 2 *Swing your right hand through to your left side. At the same time, bring your right foot through to your left side taking away your support, and so initiating your fall to your right side. Ensure that you keep your chin close to your chest. Your right foot should travel straight in front of you towards the left hand side of your body.*

Step 3 *As you land, slap the mat with your right hand. Your hand should be cupped as it makes contact. You should make contact with as much of the side of your body as possible and predominantly the thigh. Remember to turn your right foot away from the ground, thus protecting your ankle.*

Recovery

Step 1 *Slightly more difficult to perform, you are aiming to continue you movement to recover with. Raise up you right leg and, at the same time, place your left hand on the ground next to you.*

Step 2 *Follow through the motion until your right foot is on the ground and you are supported also with both of your hands.*

Step 3 *Use your hands to push back into your starting position.*

FRONT ROLLING BREAK FALL

The rolling break fall is an alternative to the front break fall and tends to lead to a softer fall because it allows the user to spread the impact out over the duration of the fall. This fall should be used when you are thrown forward. It can also be used to blend with a wrist or elbow lock (this is a common practice in aikido) and roll with it. This break fall is often seen in martial arts movies and can look really impressive, even when the stuntman is completely cooperating with the throw.

It is important to note that this break fall is not like a forward roll that is often taught in gymnastics. In the latter version, you would roll using the top of your head, or the back of your shoulders and then along your spine, along the centerline of your body. Your feet would also remain together as much as possible throughout the roll. In the break fall, you should make minimal contact with the ground using your spine. The roll will draw a line diagonally across your back from the back of your shoulder to the opposite hip.

Break Fall

Step 1 *Start in a kneeling position with your right foot and left knee on the ground. Place your right hand on your right knee. Hold your chin in towards your chest throughout the movement.*

Step 2 *Drop your weight forward and push your hands down towards the ground in front of you so that your right hand points forward and your left points back. Position your head slightly to the left, so that it is away from the side that you are going to fall on, while remembering to keep your chin down close towards your chest. Push your body weight over your shoulders and roll through, aiming to make contact with the ground with your right arm and then the back of your right shoulder. During the roll, you should feel your back coming into contact with the ground diagonally from your right shoulder towards your left hip.*

Step 3 *As you roll through, remember to slap the ground with your left cupped hand.*

Recovery

Continue through with the roll, while keeping your left foot tucked into the back of your right knee and return to your starting position.

An alternative recovery position, instead of rolling through, is to maintain a defensive posture on the ground.

From this position you can throw a sidekick up to ward off attacks.

He who hesitates, meditates in a horizontal position.

~ Ed Parker

CHAPTER EIGHT

Takedowns

This chapter presents some techniques to drop your opponent to the floor. On a hard floor, a strong throw can be every bit as damaging as a powerful strike. Judo and most karate competitions reflect this in their scoring systems, awarding points for correctly performed throws. In MMA contests, takedowns don't win fights on their own, but they are very important for ground fighters because they lead into the ground fighting phase of the fight. For a martial artist from the striking arts, knowing these maneuvers would be a handy addition to their repertoire.

SUMMARY OF TAKEDOWNS	
Hip throw	Lift an opponent onto your hip and throw them down
Shoulder throw	Lift an opponent high over your shoulder and throw them down
Outer reap	Take an opponent's legs out from under him while alongside him
Inner reap	Take an opponent's legs out from under him while pushing in to his center
Circular sacrifice throw	Defense against forward moving opponents
Side sacrifice throw	Counter to a hip or shoulder throw that drags an opponent to the ground
Double leg takedown	A maneuver that immobilizes both legs and pushes an opponent over
Single leg takedown	A maneuver that immobilizes one leg and pushes an opponent over
The sprawl	Counter to both single and double leg take downs

HIP THROW

A hip throw uses your hip as a fulcrum to lift and throw your opponent. Judo practitioners call this technique the large hip throw, *o goshi*, and use a grip on their opponent's sleeve to pull while lifting their opponent onto the hip.

Step 1 *Hold your opponent using the basic grip, with your left hand holding your opponent's right sleeve and your right hand on your opponent's lapel.*

Step 2 *Push your right hip into your opponent while, at the same time, releasing your grip with your right hand and bringing it behind your opponent's back.*

Step 3 *Continue rotating, so that you face away from your opponent, and push your hips into their body. At the same time, bend your knees so that you feel like you are getting under their body weight.*

Step 4 *Using your right arm, hold your opponent tight to your hips and lean forward slightly so that you lift their body weight onto your hips.*

Step 5 *As you take their weight off the ground, pull with your left arm and rotate your body, throwing them over your right hip. Your opponent should land on their back in front of you.*

Practical Application of the Hip Throw

In a self-defense situation, you cannot rely on your opponent having a sleeve that you can grip. Instead you need to try to grab their wrist.

Step 1 *Face your opponent in a fighting stance.*

Step 2 *As your opponent punches, block the punch.*

Step 3 *Grab your opponent's wrist and move in close, reach behind your opponent and prepare for the hip throw.*

Step 5 *Keep hold of your opponent's wrist as he lands on the ground in front of you and step over your opponent's chest with your right leg.*

Step 6 *Sit down and apply a cross arm lock, by keeping a tight hold on your opponent's wrist and leaning back.*

Step 4 *Use a hip throw to take your opponent down to the ground.*

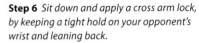

SHOULDER THROW

The shoulder throw uses your shoulder as a fulcrum to lift and throw your opponent. Judo practitioners call this a one-shoulder throw, *ippon seoi nage*, and use a grip on the jacket to help pull their opponent.

The usual way to do this throw in martial arts like judo is to grab hold of the opponent's jacket.

Step 1 *Hold your opponent using the basic grip, with your left hand holding your opponent's right sleeve and your right hand on your opponent's lapel.*

Step 2 *When you feel your opponent push you with his right arm, yield to his movement by pulling your left shoulder back and rotating so that you step in with your right shoulder. Bring your right arm under your opponent's right armpit and grab his jacket while bending your knees and pushing your hips into your opponent.*

Step 3 *Keep a tight grip on your opponents arm with your right arm and pull on his sleeve with your left hand. Lift your opponent onto your right shoulder.*

Step 4 *Twist your body so that you throw your opponent around your shoulder.*

Practical Application of the Shoulder Throw

In a self-defense situation, you cannot rely on your opponent having a jacket that you can grip. However, you can still use this throw by grabbing their wrist with one hand and grabbing under the armpit with the other.

Using this grip and by getting your weight under this point, you can still throw your opponent pushing under the armpit instead of pulling on the jacket.

Using the Shoulder Throw to Transition to Ground Fighting

You can use the shoulder throw to practice transitioning from the striking phase of combat to the ground phase. Once your opponent is on the ground you should still have a strategy for maintaining control by using a wristlock.

Step 1 *Face your opponent in fighting stance, with your left leg forward.*

Step 2 *Opponent punches with a hooking punch using his right hand. Block the punch with your left arm and, at the same time, step in with a right hook to the head.*

Step 3 *Prepare to throw, by grabbing your opponent's right wrist and reaching under his right arm.*

Step 4 *Rotate and throw your opponent over your shoulder.*

Step 5 *Keep hold of your opponent after he has landed on the ground.*

Step 6 *Apply a hyper flexing wristlock on the ground. As an extra measure of control, you can rest your left knee on his head.*

OUTER REAP

A reap takes an opponent's legs away from under him. The outer reap uses a strong leg movement. In judo, this technique is called large outside reap, *o soto gari*. Note that the outer reap comes in to take your opponent down from their outside.

Step 1 *Start with your right leg forward, using the basic grip, with your left hand hold your opponent's right sleeve and place your right hand on your opponent's lapel.*

Step 2 *Step forward with your left leg out to your left, past the outside of your opponent's right foot. At the same time, push your opponent so that he is unbalanced backwards.*

Step 3 *Step through with your right foot. Point your right foot forward, keeping your leg straight.*

Step 4 *Swing your right leg back so that you reap out your opponent's right leg. At the same time, lean forward and push your opponent's upper body back with your arms.*

Step 5 *Your opponent will be thrown to the ground on his back. You should drop your weight down ready to transition to a side control position.*

PRACTICAL APPLICATION OF THE OUTER REAP

The outer reap works well in combination with attacks that direct the opponent's weight backwards. For example, using a palm strike under your opponent's chin will tend to cause your opponent to lean back, making it easier for you to step in and use a reap to take him to the ground.

Step 1 *Face your opponent in fighting stance.*

Step 2 *As your opponent throws a hook punch at your head, block using your left arm.*

Step 3 *Use a palm strike under your opponent's chin to lift his head up and back.*

Step 4 *Step past your opponent's right side and prepare to reap.*

Step 5 *Swing your right leg back and push forwards with your right arm bringing your opponent down to the ground. You should bring your chest down on top of your opponent so that you are lying across him, pinning him and giving your access to his left arm. This will allow you to transition to an arm lock, for example an americana (see chapter 10).*

INNER REAP

Similar to the outer reap, the inner reap also takes an opponent's legs away from under him. Note that the inner reap comes in to take your opponent down from their inside.

Step 1 *Start with your right leg forward, with your left hand holding your opponent using the basic grip on the right sleeve and your right hand on your opponent's lapel.*

Step 2 *Slide in close with your right foot.*

Step 3 *Rotate so that your right shoulder is pressing against your opponent's chest, stepping through with your left foot so that it crosses behind your right.*

Step 4 *Hook your right leg behind your opponent's left and reap while pushing forward.*

CIRCULAR SACRIFICE THROW

A sacrifice throw involves sacrificing your standing position in exchange for throwing your opponent. The circular sacrifice throw, known as *tomoe nage* in judo, is best used when your opponent is moving forward to attack you and is a classic example of using your opponent's weight against him. The faster your opponent moves in to attack, the further he can be thrown.

Step 1 *Hold your opponent using the basic grip, with your left hand holding your opponent's right sleeve and your right hand high up on your opponent's lapel.*

Step 2 *As your opponent moves forward, put your right foot on his stomach and lean back so that your opponent is pulled off balance*

Step 3 *As you fall back onto the ground pulling your opponent with you, support your opponent with your foot.*

Step 4 *Catapult your opponent over the top of you.*

SIDE SACRIFICE THROW

The side sacrifice throw, known in judo as the valley drop, *tani otoshi*, is often used as a counter attack when an opponent is attempting a hip or shoulder throw. It uses your whole bodyweight to drag an opponent down to the ground.

Step 1 *Hold your opponent using the basic grip, with your left hand holding your opponent's right sleeve and your right hand on your opponent's lapel.*

Step 2 *Using a circular motion, bring your left arm round over the top of your opponent's right arm. Push in close, with your chest to your opponent's right shoulder. Reach behind his back with your left arm and grab on to his jacket or belt.*

Step 3 *Shoot your left leg out behind your opponent.*

Step 4 *Drop your weight to your left side so that your opponent is dragged backwards, falling over your left leg.*

DOUBLE LEG TAKE DOWN

This technique involves reaching in and grabbing your opponent's legs with both arms while pushing on the upper body with your shoulder or chest. This technique is sometimes called double leg shoot and in judo this is known as a two-hand reap, *morote gari.*

Step 1 *Face your opponent in a fighting stance.*

Step 2 *Bend over and charge forward, so that your arms grab round behind your opponent's knees and your shoulder pushes into his stomach.*

Step 3 *Push forward with your shoulder and pull back with your arms, bringing your opponent down to the ground.*

Practical Application of the Double Leg Takedown

It is important that you take care to setup any double leg take down, because it can be countered by striking attacks or by the sprawl.

Step 1 *Face your opponent in a fighting stance*

Step 2 *Throw punches at your opponent's head drawing his guard up.*

Step 3 *Bring your opponent down with a double leg take down.*

SINGLE LEG TAKEDOWN

One way to do a single leg take down is basically the same as the double leg takedown but only involves grabbing one leg. An alternative method is to use a technique that in judo is known as a dead tree drop, *kuchiki taoshi*.

Step 1 *Hold your opponent using the basic grip, with your left hand holding your opponent's right sleeve and your right hand on your opponent's lapel.*

Step 2 *Reach down with your left hand, under your opponent's right leg.*

Step 3 *Lift your opponent's leg, while at the same time pushing their upper body with your right hand.*

Step 4 *Keep lifting with your left arm and pushing with your right until your opponent is thrown to the ground.*

Defense Against a Clinch—Single Leg Takedown

If an opponent has you in a clinch he can throw knee strikes at your head and body. One way to escape from this and transition to ground fighting is to drop down and go for a low single leg take down. This takedown makes use of your opponent's incoming knee strike. After parrying the attack, you use it to your advantage by grabbing hold of the leg with your arms and pushing through to take your opponent down.

Step 1 *Start with your opponent holding you in the double collar tie.*

Step 2 *Use your arms to block when your opponent tries to attack with a knee strike.*

Step 3 *As your opponent's knee drops, follow it down as fast as you can and wrap your arms around his front leg.*

Step 4 *With your arms wrapped around your opponent's ankle and your shoulder pushed up tight against his shin, push forward to a low single leg takedown.*

THE SPRAWL

The sprawl is a simple but effective way to counter single and double leg takedowns. For stand-up fighters wanting to fight a grappler, this is probably the single most important technique to learn, but it is almost never taught in the striking arts such as karate or taekwondo.

The sprawl works by shooting your legs back as soon as an opponent goes in for a grab. The idea is to drop your weight onto your opponent, slamming him down into the ground. If your opponent doesn't get his elbows down to do a front break fall, then that can be a fight winner there and then. Either way, after a successful sprawl you will be in a dominant position with various possibilities open to you for acquiring a submission hold, for example, a neck hold.

Step 1 *Stand in a fighting stance with your left leg forward.*

Step 2 *As your opponent shoots in to grab your legs, shoot your legs back and drop your chest down onto your opponent's back.*

Step 3 *Grab hold of your opponent's neck.*

Step 4 *From here you would ideally transition to rear control and attempt a rear naked choke (see chapter 10).*

When in doubt, choke him out!

~ Gene Lebell

CHAPTER NINE

Locks and Choke Holds

A joint lock is a grappling technique that applies force to a joint in a direction that is contrary to the joint's normal direction of motion or beyond its natural range of motion. A joint lock is usually applied during ground fighting, but it can also be used while standing up, particularly in a self-defense context.

In competitions, joint locks are a way to get your opponent to submit by hyper-extending, hyper-rotating, or hyper-flexing their joints. In a self-defense situation, joint locks can be used to restrain an opponent or, if necessary, pressure can be brought to bear on the joint to the point where there could be tendon and ligament damage, or possibly even a dislocation or bone fracture. It is therefore important that, when practicing these techniques with a sparring partner, that they only be applied gradually, allowing the receiver to submit. Martial artists signal this either verbally, for example, by saying "I submit," or by tapping the ground or their own body several times. For this reason, submitting is often referred to as "tapping out." Because of the potential dangers of joint locks, it is essential that you be ready to release the lock immediately when your partner taps out. Just as important, if your sparring partner holds you in a joint lock, you should not be stubborn and refuse to tap out despite feeling your joint lock out.

There are many types of locks, but in competitions, many types of locks are not allowed. This will vary from one competition to the next but usually only locks applied to the elbow joint are allowed.

A chokehold is a grappling move that restricts breathing or blood flow by constricting the neck. These techniques can induce unconsciousness or even death and so must be used with caution.

SUMMARY OF LOCKS AND HOLDS	
Arm lock	A joint lock that hyper-extends the elbow
Cross arm lock	A joint lock that can be used during ground fighting
Americana	An arm lock that can be used during ground fighting
The Kimura	A shoulder lock
Rear naked choke	A choke that can be used from the rear mount
Cross choke	A choke that can be used from the mount
Supinating wrist lock	A lock wrist lock that can be used as a submission technique in a standing position
Pronating wrist lock	A wrist lock that can be used as a submission technique in a standing position
Hyperflexing wrist lock	A wrist lock that can be used as a pain compliance technique

ARM LOCK

An arm lock, also known as an arm bar, works by applying pressure against the wrist and elbow in opposite directions. Continued application of this pressure will cause pain and will lead your opponent to submit. Further continuation of this pressure will hyper-extend the arm and could result in a serious injury.

To apply an armlock, push up on the elbow and pull down on the wrist. You can use a circular motion to apply an arm lock while standing.

Step 1 *Your opponent grabs your right wrist with his right hand.*

Step 2 *Push your right hand out slightly to the left hand side.*

Step 3 *Keep your right hand moving up to the left while pushing on your opponent's left elbow with your left hand. As you move your right hand, rotate your wrist so that you can grab your opponent's wrist with your right hand.*

Step 4 *Get a firm grip on your opponent's wrist and pull it to your right hip. At the same time, push on your opponent's elbow. The idea is to straighten your opponent's arm so that you can apply an arm lock.*

CROSS ARM LOCK

This technique is also known as "cross arm breaker" or "crucifix arm bar." In judo, this is called *juji gatame* and it is the most successful submission technique in that sport. It is also a very common submission technique in MMA and wrestling.

Step 1 *Start on top of your opponent in the mount position.*

Step 2 *As your opponent reaches up to your neck, pass your left arm under his right arm and your right arm over his left arm to press down on his body.*

Step 3 *Push your weight forward and bring your left foot up to your opponent's right hip.*

Step 4 *Rotate yourself by bringing your right knee alongside your opponent's left ear.*

Step 5 *Bring your right foot around to the other side of your opponent's head and hug your opponent's left arm.*

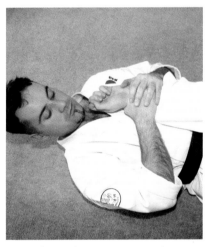

Ensure that you keep your opponent's arm straight with his thumb on top.

Step 6 *Lie back, keeping a strong hold on your opponent's left arm. Pull back on your opponents forearm and lift your hips so that you apply an arm bar. Some people use their groin to apply the pressure to the elbow joint but it is also possible to angle your body slightly so that the elbow contact point is on your thigh.*

AMERICANA

This arm lock is also known as the four-figure arm lock. In judo, this is called an arm entanglement, *ude garami*.

The Americana in Ground Fighting

Step 1 *Start in the mount position.*

Step 2 *Grab your opponent's left wrist with your left hand and pin it on the ground, putting your left elbow next to your opponent's head.*

Step 3 *Reach under your opponent's left elbow with your right hand and grab hold of your left wrist.*

Step 4 *Bring your opponent's elbow down towards your hip while at the same time lifting his elbow away from the ground with your right forearm until your opponent submits.*

Your opponent can escape from this technique by rolling you over onto your right side. You can prevent this by hooking your left leg under your opponent's right leg and keeping your right knee out to the side to act as a solid base.

The Americana as a Takedown Technique

You can also use the americana as a takedown technique from a standing position.

Step 1 *Face your opponent in fighting stance with your left leg forward.*

Step 2 *As your opponent punches with a left jab, deflect it with a high level block using your left arm.*

Step 3 *Grab your opponent's wrist with your left hand and strike with a knife hand strike to your opponent's temple using your right hand.*

Step 5 *Slide forward so that you pass your opponent on their left side while rotating his forearm by pushing his elbow to your left and his wrist to your right.*

Step 6 *Drop your weight by bending your knees, so that your opponent is forced down to the ground.*

Step 4 *Bring your right hand back to the inside of your opponent's left elbow while you push opponent's wrist forward using your left hand, so that your opponent's arm bends at the elbow. Grab your own left wrist with your right hand.*

THE KIMURA

This shoulder lock was nicknamed "the kimura" after the great judo master, Masahiko Kimura, after he used it to defeat Helio Gracie in a no holds barred fight in 1951. It is also called a key lock because to apply it you twist the upper arm like turning a key in a lock. In judo, this technique is called *ude-garami*. It is somewhat like the Americana but is applied behind the opponent's back.

Step 1 *Start in the full guard position (as shown in Chapter 11) with your opponent on top of you.*

Step 2 *Take hold of your opponent's left hand and put it down on the mat next to you.*

Step 3 *As a transition to the next position, change to the open guard so that you can lift yourself up and move your hips to the left and rotate a bit to face to the right. Reach around the outside of your opponent's left elbow with your left arm, reaching through under his arm so that you can grab your own right wrist. Lean back and lift your opponent's left hand, bending his arm.*

Step 4 *Bring your opponent's arm behind his back. Put your right foot in the middle of your opponent's back, so that your opponent cannot escape. Bring your opponent's wrist towards his head until your opponent submits.*

REAR NAKED CHOKE

This technique is also known as the "sleeper hold" because it can render an opponent unconscious if applied for more than a few seconds. This works by restricting blood flow to the brain. In order to do this, you need to make sure that you are applying it to the correct part of the neck. If you apply pressure to the front, on your opponent's throat, then you will be constricting their airway. This can cause damage to the windpipe and, although this will eventually cause unconsciousness, it will take some time. It is far better to apply pressure to the side of the neck so that you restrict blood flow through the carotid artery that supplies blood to the brain. If applied correctly, this will cause unconsciousness in less than 10 seconds.

This technique can be applied against a standing opponent but it is usually not possible to get into this position against a ready opponent, so this choke is most commonly used during ground fighting.

Step 1 *Start with your opponent kneeling in front of you, facing away from you.*

Step 2 *Put your left hand on your opponent's left shoulder. Reach around your opponent's neck with your right arm, so that your right forearm is under your opponent's chin and your right hand reaches to your left hand. Keep in tight to your opponent – don't give him space to head butt you.*

Step 3 *Slide your arm under your right hand and snake your left hand up over your right arm and then behind your opponent's head. You should be able to touch your right shoulder with your left hand. To apply the choke, squeeze by pulling with your biceps.*

CROSS CHOKE

Like the rear naked choke, this technique can be used to submit or knock out an opponent by constricting the carotid artery. In judo, this technique is called the cross lock, *juji jime*. This technique requires that the opponent wears a heavy jacket, such as that worn in judo or jujutsu, this is what's used to pull against when applying pressure.

Step 1 *Start in the mount position, sitting on your opponent's stomach.*

Step 2 *With your right hand, grab high up on the collar of your opponent's jacket. With your left hand, reach under your right arm to the other side of the collar.*

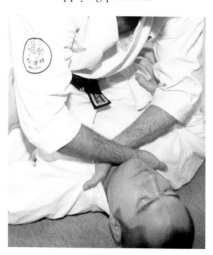

Step 3 *Pull your elbows out so that the bones of your forearms press into the side of your opponent's neck.*

This technique works equally well from the guard position.

Step 1 *Start in the closed guard position.*

Step 2 *Using your legs, pull your opponent in close to you.*

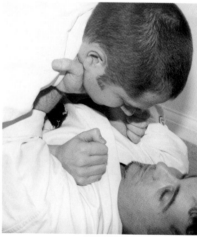

Step 3 *Apply the cross choke.*

SUPINATING WRISTLOCK

In jujutsu, this technique is called a forearm return, *kote gaeshi* and is one of the most common wristlocks in the martial arts. In aikido, this technique is also called *sankyo* which means "third one," It works by applying a torque to the wrist joint, which does not have any rotational mobility and so causes a rotation (supination) in the radioulnar joint. Its most common use is to force an opponent to the ground, but in a self-defense situation it could be used to dislocate the shoulder or break the wrist.

Step 1 *Start with your opponent gripping your jacket with his right hand.*

Step 2 *Rotate your body to your right. With your left hand, reach over the top of your opponent's right hand and grab it placing your thumb on the back of his hand and wrapping your fingers around the base of his thumb.*

Step 3 *Step forwards past your opponent's right side while peeling your opponent's hand back away from you, rotating it anticlockwise. Use your right hand to assist with this movement by grabbing the other side of your opponent's hand, placing your right thumb on the back of his and and wrapping your fingers around the blade of his hand.*

Step 4 *Use both hands to push your opponent's wrist back so that his fingers go back to his right.*

PRONATING WRISTLOCK

In jujutsu, this technique is called a forearm rotation, *kote mawashi*. It is similar to the supinating wristlock but rotates in the opposite direction (pronation). Unlike the supinating wristlock, it does not work if your opponent is allowed to straighten his arm because keeping the elbow joint bent reduces the range of rotation.

Step 1 *Start facing your opponent in fighting stance with your left leg forward.*

Step 2 *Use both arms to block as your opponent attacks with a left hook.*

Step 3 *Grab hold of your opponent's left wrist with your right hand and pull him forward to help break his balance.*

Step 4 *Keep hold of your opponent's wrist while ducking under his left arm. Come alongside him with your right shoulder next to his left. While maintaining your grip, your thumb and forefinger should be wrapped around your opponent's wrist like pincers while the rest of your fingers run along the blade of his hand. Ensure that your opponent's elbow remains high so that you can apply the wristlock.*

Step 5 *Grab with your right hand as if shaking the hand. Apply the wristlock by rotating your opponent's wrist clockwise.*

HYPER FLEXING WRISTLOCK

This technique is also known as the chicken wing or gooseneck. It hyper flexes the wrist joint by pushing the hand towards the forearm. This technique is often used as a pain compliance technique by law enforcement agents or for self-defense. Once you have this lock in place, it is relatively easy to control the movements of the subject of the lock.

Step 1 *Stand standing alongside your opponent with your right shoulder next to his left shoulder.*

Step 2 *Grab your opponent's left wrist with your left hand and put your right arm under your opponent's left armpit.*

Step 3 *Lift your opponent's wrist with your left arm while cutting down into their elbow with your right hand so that your bend their left elbow.*

Step 4 *Use both hands to bend your opponent's wrist to hyper flex the wrist.*

"The dance of battle is always played to the same impatient rhythm. What begins in a surge of violent motion is always reduced to the perfectly still."

~ *Sun Tzu*

CHAPTER TEN

Ground Fighting

The next chapter looks at things you can do after you have your opponent on the ground. To the casual observer, ground fighting can look like a clumsy mess of mass and muscle. But to the expert ground fighter, the process of maneuvering, pinning, and submitting an opponent is at least as complex tactically as any stand up fight.

On the ground there are essentially four places that you can find yourself:

To the side: This is a good position from which to apply a submission hold. Techniques that are used from this position are called side control techniques.

At your opponent's feet: From this position your opponent will be in a guard position, using his feet to keep you away. You need to get past his guard to a side or mount position.

On top of your opponent: This is a mount position. From here you can strike your opponent or apply a submission.

Behind your opponent: This is generally considered the best position to be in. From here your opponent cannot do much to hurt you, but you can apply a chokehold.

On your back: Either your opponent is on top of you in a mount position, or you are in a guard position. From here you will want to improve your position and get your opponent onto his back.

SUMMARY OF LOCKS AND HOLDS	
Side four-corner hold	A side control technique that can pin an opponent to the ground
Scarf hold	A side control technique that can pin an opponent to the ground
Shoulder hold	A side control technique that can pin or strangle an opponent
Chest hold	A side control technique that can be used as a chokehold
Guard	A defensive posture used when you are on your back
Mount	A dominant position used when you are on top of an opponent
Back mount	A dominant position with your opponent facing away from you
Escaping the high mount	A technique to improve your position
Passing the guard	Getting past an opponent's defenses to apply a submission technique

SIDE FOUR-CORNER HOLD

In judo, this side control technique is called *yoko shiho gatame.* In a judo contest, this can be used to simply pin an opponent. In other situations, it is more common to transition to a mount position or to a submission hold such as a scarf hold or an arm bar. It is a useful position to assume because it allows you time to regain your breath while using your body weight to restrict your opponent's breathing. This allows you to recover while tiring your opponent out before you transition into a submission move.

Step 1 *Start with your opponent lying on his back. Kneel on his right hand side, facing towards his chest.*

Step 2 *Put your chest down on your opponent's chest and reach around underneath his neck and grab onto his collar. Put your right arm around his left thigh and grab on to his belt or trousers.*

CHEST HOLD

In judo, this side control technique is called *mune gatame.*

Step 1 *Start with your opponent lying on his back. Kneel on his right hand side, facing towards his chest.*

Step 2 *Put your chest down on your opponent's chest and reach around underneath his neck and then under his back towards his left shoulder. With your right arm, reach over the left side of his chest and try to grab hold of your own left hand.*

SCARF HOLD

In judo, this side control technique is called *kesa gatame*. It is called the scarf hold because you wrap your arm around your opponent's neck like a scarf. You can use this move to tire your opponent by putting your weight on his chest making it difficult for him to breathe.

Step 1 *Start with your opponent lying on his back. Sit with your back against the right side of his body.*

Step 2 *Lean over your opponent's chest and put your right arm under the back of his neck. Secure this position by grabbing the right shoulder of his jacket.*

Step 3 *Hold your opponents right arm with your left. Keep your legs spread out to maintain stability. Keep your head down close to your opponent's head to avoid him grabbing you under the chin and pulling you back.*

SHOULDER HOLD

The shoulder hold is a side control technique similar to the scarf hold but traps an arm alongside your opponent's neck. Like the scarf hold, this can be used as a pin but it can also be used as a chokehold, squeezing your opponent's arm against his own neck. In judo this technique is called *kata gatame*.

Step 1 *Start with your opponent lying on his back. Sit with your back against the right side of his body.*

Step 2 *Lean over your opponent's chest and put your right arm under the back of his neck. Secure this position by grabbing the right shoulder of his jacket.*

Step 3 *Lift your opponent's right arm up and push your head up against the outside of his arm. Squeeze your head and right arm closer together, applying the chokehold.*

ESCAPING THE CHEST HOLD

Once the chest hold is fully applied it is almost impossible to escape. However, you can escape from the chest hold if you get the opportunity to work your hand through into the center under your opponent. From there you can push your opponent up and work on reversing the hold.

Step 1 *Lie on your back with your opponent lying on your right side applying a chest hold.*

Step 2 *Push up your opponent's chest with your left hand.*

Step 3 *Slip your right hand in, under your opponent's chest.*

Step 4 *Using both arms, push your opponent up to create more space and then reach over his left shoulder with your right arm and grab your own right leg.*

Step 5 *Using your legs as a counter weight, sit up, rolling your opponent.*

Step 6 *Keep rolling your opponent until he is on his back and you have side control using a scarf hold.*

GUARD

This is a position on the ground from which the person on the bottom can utilize a number of submission techniques including arm bars and chokes. In judo, this is called *do-osae*, which means "trunk hold." There are a few variations on the guard position.

Closed Guard *In the closed guard (also known as the full guard), your legs are wrapped around your opponent's waist and your ankles are locked behind his back.*

Butterfly guard *In the butterfly guard, your knees are still bent but your feet are pressed into your opponent's hips.*

Open Guard *In the open guard your knees are bent but your feet are flat on the ground. In this position it is easier for your opponent to either get up or to pass the guard so it should only be used as a temporary position to allow you to transition to a submission move.*

Half Guard *The half guard is similar to the closed guard but you only have one of your opponent's legs entangled. In this position, your opponent is said to be in half mount and will attempt to transition to either side control or to a full mount position.*

Rubber Guard *The rubber guard traps your opponent's neck and one of his arms using your legs. You should lock your legs by hooking the ankle of one leg behind the bent knee of the other leg.*

MOUNT

In the mount position, you sit on your opponent's chest. From this position, you can use arm locks and chokes but against an experienced opponent this is surprisingly difficult. You can lift yourself up and then strike while your opponent is unable to retaliate in kind, because he is unable to put his weight behind any strikes. In MMA, this is called "ground and pound".

Step 1 *In the low mount position you sit on your opponent's stomach.*

Step 3 *Use strikes to attack your opponent.*

Step 2 *Lift yourself up ready to strike. If you do this by pushing down hard on your opponent's stomach, you can wind them giving you a better opportunity to attack.*

Training Tips

A good defense against this tactic is for the person on the ground to lift up his hips. This will throw the mounted attacker off balance.

The high mount offers a better opportunity to strike. Assume the high mount by moving forwards so that you are sitting on your opponent's chest rather than his stomach.

Your opponent will now be unable to throw you off balance with his hips because you will be positioned too far above his hips.

BACK MOUNT

In the back mount (also known as the rear mount), you are behind your opponent, with your arms around your opponent's neck or torso and your legs hooking through over your opponent's thighs. From this position, you can apply chokes and arm bars while also being able to attack with punches or elbow strikes.

If done correctly, it is very difficult for an opponent to escape from the back mount. No matter how your opponent moves, you will still be on his back and able to attack him.

Training Tips

When you are in the rear mount position do not cross your legs.

If you cross your ankles over, then your opponent can apply a "figure four "leg lock.

ESCAPING A HIGH MOUNT

While your opponent is on top of you, he is in a dominant position and can rain down strikes on you. It is therefore very important to be able to escape from this position. One way to do this is to use a sweep that topples your opponent and reverses the position, allowing you to take the dominant position.

Step 1 *Lie on your back with your opponent in a high mount.*

Step 2 *Brace your elbows against your opponent's knees and use them to wriggle up, so that your opponent is then in a low mount.*

Step 3 *Grab your opponent's right hand. If you do not trap your opponent's hand then he will be able to use it to brace himself and stop you from sweeping him over.*

Step 4 *Use your left foot to trap your opponent's right foot, by moving your foot closer to your body on the outside of your opponent's foot. Bring your right foot as close up near to your body as you can. This gives you the leverage to left your opponent and topple him over.*

Step 5 *Push off your right foot, lift your hips, and roll your opponent over to the side. As you rotate over, it is important to shoot your hands out to the side to stop the roll when you are on top, otherwise your opponent will be able to continue the roll and return to the dominant top position.*

PASSING THE GUARD

If your opponent is a guard position and you want to proceed to a side control position or mount position, you will have to do what is known as "passing the guard."

Step 1 *Your opponent starts in the butterfly guard.*

Step 2 *Push you right shoulder forward down to your opponent's stomach. Straighten your right leg behind you.*

Step 3 *Push your opponent's left foot down onto the ground.*

Step 4 *Jump over your opponent's left knee, so that you land on your knees on his left hand side.*

Step 5 *Move your right arm under your opponent's neck to achieve side control.*

If your opponent is in the closed guard, then passing the guard is a bit harder, especially if he is holding on very tightly.

Step 1 *Your opponent starts in the closed guard.*

Step 2 *Squeeze your right arm in between your opponent's left leg and the right side of your body.*

Step 3 *Using your right arm, lift your opponent's left leg up onto your shoulder.*

Step 4 *Push your weight forward onto your opponent's leg and rotate round anticlockwise, so that you come round to your opponent's side and assume a side control position.*

*Prepare yourself for the world, as the athletes used
to do for their exercise; oil your mind and your
manners, to give them the necessary suppleness
and flexibility; strength alone will not do.*

~ Lord Chesterfield

CHAPTER ELEVEN

Stretching for the Martial Artist

Training in the martial arts and working towards your goals, whether that is to be a black belt or to be a fighting champion, requires a long-term commitment. It becomes a lifestyle choice for many, rather than just being a hobby that they take part in occasionally. It is inspirational to see many martial arts master in their sixties and beyond still in such good physical state. This alone can encourage students to stick to their training regime for the longer term.

Some students train in the martial arts simply as a way to stay active, supple, and healthy into the later years of their lives. For this reason, having a balanced understanding of other aspects, such as stretching, can result in benefits over the longer term. Many instructors and students know that these aspects are important from an overall fitness point of view. However, putting these convictions into practice is a much harder thing to do. Like dieting or exercising, you know it's good for you but taking control and implementing is so much harder. Indeed, it is much easier to do lots of training under an instructor, no matter how tough, compared to working individually to improve your diet and overall well being.

In this chapter, a variety of stretching exercises are described that can be used to help improve your technique and performance in your chosen martial art. The most obvious example is stretching to improve the flexibility of your legs in order to help you to perform better kicks. Stretching can also help to extend your normal range of motion. This can, in turn, help to reduce the risk of injury as your muscles will be used to going through a much larger range of motion then they would otherwise experience. Range of motion is also important in ground fighting where it is sometimes necessary to contort your body in order to apply or to escape a hold.

Leg Flexibility

When martial artists think of stretching, they tend to mostly think about what they can do to improve their leg flexibility. The objective is to improve their kicks through the development of their body. In particular, this is an important part of taekwondo training, where flashy high kicks are a key part of training. Karate also has an emphasis on kicks, although to a lesser degree than in taekwondo. Therefore, taekwondo students tend to be more committed to flexibility training than karate students. The important thing to note is that improving your flexibility will impact all aspects of your life and not just your martial arts training and so have to decide how important this is for you. As people often say, if you knew how you would feel when you were older then you would make more of an effort to stay healthy and fit when you were younger.

In all stretches, and in particular the leg stretches, which students normally find the hardest, it is important try to hold the position for increasing amounts of time. Practicing stretching several times a week and incorporating simple stretching exercises into your everyday life will take the pain out of making the commitment.

LEG STRETCHES
Forward lunge stretch
Standing forward bend
Sitting forward bend
Horse riding stance stretch
Standing hip adductor stretch
Sitting hip adductor stretch
Simple quadriceps stretch
Advanced quadriceps stretch
Gluteals stretch
Simple calves stretch
Advanced calves stretch

FORWARD LUNGE STRETCH

This stretch takes advantage of a common stance used in martial arts. It is an extension of the normal forward stance, where most of your weight is over your leading leg. Your back should remain upright during this exercise. This exercise works the hamstrings and the calves and is the first step towards the front splits, also known as the scissor splits. This flexibility is useful for improving your technique for high front kicks and strong back kicks.

Step 1 *Stand with your feet hip width apart.*

Step 2 *Take one large step forward and then lower your weight such that your front leg is parallel to the ground. Keep your upper body relaxed while you hold this position.*

STANDING FORWARD BEND

This exercise works the hamstrings in both legs at the same time. It also gives the back a good stretch. If you find that you cannot reach the ground, then just go as far as you can and hold.

Step 1 *Stand with your feet hip width apart.*

Step 2 *Keep your upper body relaxed and reach towards your toes by bending at your hips. Your legs must remain straight throughout this stretch.*

Step 3 *If you can, continue your reach towards the ground and then rest your palms flat on the ground. If you cannot reach the ground then just hold with your fingers pointing towards the ground.*

SITTING FORWARD BEND

A seated version of the previous exercise works the same muscles, namely the back of the legs and the back. You may find this version a little bit harder. Do not be tempted to strain your neck or back in this exercise.

Step 1 *Sit on the ground with your feet hip width apart and your back straight.*

Step 2 *Bend forward at your hips and reach towards your toes.*

Step 3 *If you can, continue to reach forward to get hold of you feet and then rest your head down on your knees.*

HORSE RIDING STANCE STRETCH

This exercise makes use of a side stance that is called horse-riding stance in karate and kung fu. Once you get into this position, you will need to focus on keeping your body low and to not be tempted to gradually lift up to reduce the stretch. Karate students sometimes practice upper body moves, like punches and blocks, whilst in this position in order to help take their mind off the stretch. This stretch works the inside of the legs intensely and is useful in training towards the side splits, also known as the box splits. This flexibility can help you improve your technique for side-kicks and circular kicks.

Step 1 *Stand with your feet two hip widths apart.*

Step 2 *Keeping your feet parallel to each other and drop your weight by bending at the knees. Ensure that your knees are pushed outwards.*

Step 3 *If you can, lower your weight even further such that your legs are closer to being parallel to the ground.*

STANDING HIP ADDUCTOR STRETCH

This exercise also works the inside legs intensely. This standing version makes use of your weight to help increase the stretch. This is a good exercise for those aspiring to be able to do the side splits.

Step 1 *Stand with your legs as wide apart as possible and with both feet pointing forward.*

Step 2 *Bend at the hips and reach towards the ground with your hands. Place your palms flat on the ground if you can reach.*

Step 3 *From this position, you can work towards achieving the wide splits by slowly pushing your feet further apart. With practice, you should become more comfortable and be able to push further.*

SITTING HIP ADDUCTOR STRETCH

This is a seated version of the previous exercise and is a little more difficult to perform as it does not use your weight in your favor. However, it does enable you to have a little more control over the extent of the stretch.

Step 1 *Sit on the ground with your legs as wide apart as possible but do not bend your knees. Keep your back straight.*

Step 2 *Keep your upper body relaxed and place your palms on the ground in front of you if you can reach.*

Step 3 *Slowly push your hands forward and use the motion to bring your upper body closer to the ground.*

SIMPLE QUADRICEPS STRETCH

The quadriceps muscle group is one that often gets missed during training. However, if you are working on your hamstrings, then you'll need to make sure that you balance your training by also working on the other side of your leg. This is a simple exercise that can be used to punctuate your other training. Flexible quadriceps are required to be able to perform the front splits.

Step 1 *Stand with your feet hip width apart.*

Step 2 *Raise one leg behind you by bending at your knee and hold your leg with both hands and pull your leg in as close to your body as possible.*

ADVANCED QUADRICEPS STRETCH

This exercise is more advanced than the previous exercise, and thus works the quadriceps more intensely. You should attempt this exercise after you feel that you are not gaining much from the previous exercise. Again, this exercise is a good one for those training towards achieving the front splits.

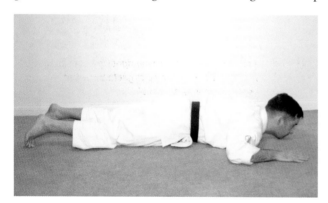

Step 1 *Lie on the ground face down.*

Step 2 *Raise your legs behind you by bending at the knees.*

Step 3 *Reach around to get hold of your legs with your hands.*

GLUTEALS STRETCH

This muscle group often gets missed in training and yet these muscles can be really tight and working on their flexibility can help the overall performance of your kicks. This exercise effectively isolates certain muscles.

Step 1 *Lie on the ground face up and bend your knees with your feet flat on the ground.*

Step 2 *Place your left ankle on the other knee.*

Step 3 *Lift your right foot off the ground to that your knee moves towards you.*

Step 4 *With your hands, reach around your right leg just below the knee and slowly pull towards you, aiming to get the knee of the leg you are holding as close to your body as possible.*

SIMPLE CALVES STRETCH

This exercise is good at effectively working the calves. You should feel an intense stretch across this muscle when performing this exercise.

Step 1 *Stand with your feet hip width apart and two feet away from a wall.*

Step 2 *Place your hands on the wall and lean forward while keeping your entire body straight. Try to keep your heels on the ground.*

Step 3 *To increase the stretch, try standing further away from the wall.*

ADVANCED CALVES STRETCH

This exercise builds on the previous one, so attempt this one after you are comfortable with the simple version.

Step 1 *Stand with your feet one in front of the other.*

Step 2 *Keep your upper body relaxed and lower your upper body by bending at the hips.*

Step 3 *If you can reach, place your palms flat on the ground just in front of your feet.*

Arm Flexibility

Upper body techniques such as punches and blocks obviously use the arms. However, these exercises are also useful for martial arts that involve locks and holds, where your joints and limbs may be contorted. Having flexible muscles should help to reduce the risk of injury. In particular, these will be useful for karate, kung fu, jujutsu, and aikido.

ARM STRETCHES
Arms behind back stretch
Arms rotation
Wrist flexor
Wrist extensor
Forearm rotation

ARMS BEHIND THE BACK STRETCH

This exercise works the arms and shoulders intensely. Working on this exercise should eventually enable you to reach any part of your back.

Position your arms behind your back with one arm going over the top and one going from underneath. Bring your hands closer together and if you can reach, interlock your hands together.

If you cannot reach, then you can hold a towel in your hands to help you to bring your hands as close together as possible.

ARMS ROTATION

This simple exercise is good for using your range of motion and keeping you in good condition.

Step 1 *Hold your arms out to either side.*

Step 2 *Rotate your arms, marking your circles as big as you possibly can.*

WRIST FLEXOR

This exercise is useful for any martial arts that use the wrists, for example, the palm hand strike in karate and the pressure put on these joints through wristlock exercises.

Step 1 *Hold one of your arms our straight in front of you.*

Step 2 *Using your other hand, pull the palm back with the palm facing away from you.*

WRIST EXTENSOR

This is another useful exercise for preparing your wrists for training involving wrist rotations and locks.

Step 1 *Hold one of your arms out straight in front of you.*

Step 2 *Using your other hand, pull the palm back with the palm facing towards you.*

FOREARM ROTATION

This is the motion that your forearm goes through when a supinating wristlock is applied on you and so this is a useful stretch for warming up before practicing this type of wristlock. This movement is often wrongly attributed to the wrists, but, in fact, it is the entire forearm that is turning.

Step 1 *Hold your right hand out in front of you with your palm facing towards you.*

Step 2 *With your left hand, reach behind your right hand and grab your thumb.*

Step 3 *Rotate your right wrist so that your thumb moves away from you.*

Back Flexibility

The back comprises of numerous muscles and it is an essential part of all of your techniques. It is central to your development as a martial artist and should not be neglected.

SIMPLE LOWER BACK STRETCH

In this exercise, you start in a standard press up position. From there you lift your upper body, arching the lower back, thus giving you a stretch in this area.

BACK STRETCHES
Simple lower backstretch
Advanced lower backstretch
Trapezius stretch
Backstretch
Spinal rotation

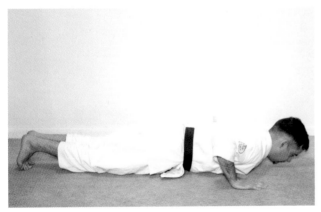

Step 1 *Lie on the ground face down with your palms on the ground in line with your shoulders.*

Step 2 *Keeping your hips on the ground, lift your upper body off the ground.*

ADVANCED LOWER BACK STRETCH

Attempt this exercise after you are comfortable with the previous one. In addition to working the back intensely, it also requires upper body strength to hold yourself up.

Step 1 *Lie on the ground face up.*

Step 2 *Place your hands on the ground near your head.*

Step 3 *Lift your body up by bringing your hands and your feet closer together.*

TRAPEZIUS STRETCH

This is a simple yet effective exercise for working the trapezius. This muscles comes down from the side of the head and over the shoulder.

Step 1 *Look straight ahead and relax your shoulders.*

Step 2 *Bend your head to one side, bringing your ear closer to your shoulder. Repeat for the other side.*

BACK STRETCH

This exercise gives a good lengthening feeling and provides an opening stretch across the back. This is quite an invigorating stretch.

Step 1 *Stand with your feet hip width apart.*

Step 2 *Raise your arms above your head. Reach as high as you can but do not let your heels come off the ground.*

SPINAL ROTATION

This exercise works the muscles in the middle of the back and also the sides of your body. This is quite a relaxing stretch.

Step 1 *Stand with your feet hip width apart and your elbows held out to the side.*

Step 2 *Keep your feet where they are and rotate your body around as far as you can so that you can see behind you.*

*The wise man should consider that health
is the greatest of human blessings.
Let food be your medicine.*

~ Hippocrates

CHAPTER TWELVE

Nutrition for the Martial Artist

Martial artists can be interested in nutrition for a variety of reasons. Perhaps they started training in martial arts as part of their efforts to lose weight or to build muscle. Or perhaps they want to just supplement their training with an overall healthy and balanced lifestyle. Whatever the reason, a basic grounding in sports nutrition can help you to make the most of your training as well as improve your general well being.

Understanding some basics about nutrition can help you to be better prepared for long and demanding training sessions or even help you to be ready for competitions, helping to ensure that you have the required energy and hydration levels to ensure optimum performance. Described here are some simple tips on what foods and drinks you can keep in your training bag that will help you make the most of your training. In addition, some basics of weight management and eating to gain muscle mass are explained.

It makes sense to eat food that provides us with all the nutrients our bodies need—but what exactly is a balanced diet? Which foods contribute most to our well being? Should we avoid certain foods altogether? It is recommended that we eat fruit and vegetables from a wide selection every day. These are the foods that provide us with the fiber, minerals, essential vitamins, folic acid, and carotene that keep our body in good working order. With active lifestyles, it is difficult to eat well. Often we find it frustrating when trying to have a healthy eating plan as well as working, studying, and exercising.

Although people now take more time to exercise, they still do not, or do not know how to eat correctly. If there is a deficiency or imbalance in any particular nutrient, then there will eventually be a negative side effect, be it low energy or poor health. Nutrients are taken in by the body for energy and to maintain and build body tissue. No single food provides all the nutrients required for the body to remain healthy and work properly. All foods provide some nutrients and contribute to taste, smell, color, texture, and enjoyment of the meal. Choosing foods for a healthy diet does not mean giving up favorites. Simply try to enjoy a wide variety of foods in the proportions shown on the food pyramid.

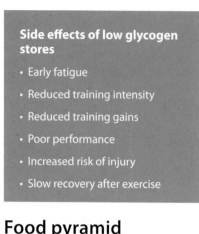

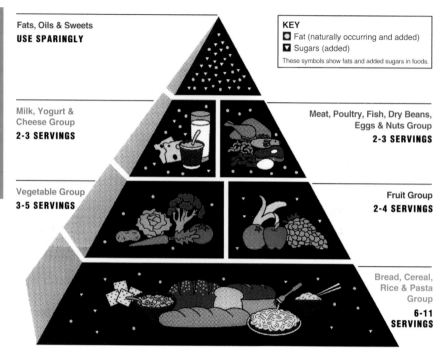

Side effects of low glycogen stores

- Early fatigue
- Reduced training intensity
- Reduced training gains
- Poor performance
- Increased risk of injury
- Slow recovery after exercise

Fats, Oils & Sweets
USE SPARINGLY

KEY
- ☐ Fat (naturally occurring and added)
- ▼ Sugars (added)

These symbols show fats and added sugars in foods.

Milk, Yogurt & Cheese Group
2-3 SERVINGS

Meat, Poultry, Fish, Dry Beans, Eggs & Nuts Group
2-3 SERVINGS

Vegetable Group
3-5 SERVINGS

Fruit Group
2-4 SERVINGS

Bread, Cereal, Rice & Pasta Group
6-11 SERVINGS

Food pyramid

Good nutrition leads to:
- good health and good muscle development
- good posture and smooth skin
- a normal appetite and an improved immune system

Carbohydrates

Carbohydrates provide the body with energy and are stored as glycogen in the muscles and liver with 3 times their weight in water, and so low carbohydrate diets can lead to quick weight (water!) loss. A lack can lead to low energy and fatigue, whereas taking in excess carbohydrates can lead to laying down fat. Simple carbohydrates are dried fruit, fresh fruit and sugar. Complex carbohydrates are potatoes, rice, bread, pasta, starches, and cereals. 66% of your calorie intake should be carbohydrate.

Fiber

Fiber is indigestible carbohydrate. It absorbs water in the digestive tract, making the food contents bulkier and easier to pass through the body. It also decreases the amount of time that food waste spends inside the body by stimulating peristalsis and thus reduces the risk of infection. Increasing fiber in the diet causes a slowing down of the absorption of sugar into the blood, aiding the slow release of energy and helping to reduce cholesterol. A fiber poor diet can lead to constipation, diabetes, and other digestive system disorders.

SOURCES OF FIBER

Eating more fruit and vegetables is one of the most important things we can do to improve our health, reducing the risk of heart disease, cancer and strokes. They are naturally low in fat and sodium and provide a good amount of fiber. Choose a wide variety of colors and types to ensure you are getting a balance of nutrients. It is important to choose more from rich starchy foods, such as whole meal grains and cereals, pasta and rice. Besides providing us with energy, they are good sources of fiber, B vitamins, calcium and iron. For extra fiber try whole meal, whole grain, and brown alternatives. Adding bran, however, to a nutrient poor diet is not advisable, as it reduces the absorption of essential nutrients, including zinc.

Glycaemic Index

The body can only store a small amount of glycogen at any one time. The total store in the average body amounts to about 1600-2000 kcal. This is only enough to last one day if you didn't eat anything. This is why a low carbohydrate diet makes people lose a lot of weight in the first few days. The weight loss is almost entirely due to the loss of glycogen and water - and not fat. A carbohydrate's effect on blood sugar level is determined by its glycaemic response, which is its ability to contribute glucose into the blood stream. Carbohydrates are the best choice for refueling muscles and promoting good health.

The glycaemic index concept was originally designed to help people with diabetes to control their blood sugar level. This index is not accurate for foods when they are mixed together, but for athletes who often use only one type of food to fuel themselves, this index has become very useful. By ranking foods (on a scale that goes up to 100 where absorption is effectively immediate) according to their ability to elevate blood sugar, nutritional professionals have developed a glycaemic index (GI).

This index is useful when choosing the right foods for different occasions. Generally, you require quick absorption immediately before exercise, during and in the two hours following exercise. And, you require slow absorption 2-4 hours before exercise and the recovery period between exercising.

A food's glycaemic index is influenced by many factors including:
- the amount eaten
- fiber content, added fat and added protein decrease blood sugar level
- starch type
- cooking and processing of food

QUICK GUIDE TO LOW, MEDIUM AND HIGH GLYCAEMIC INDEX (GI) FOODS	
High GI foods	White and whole meal bread, white and brown rice, cornflakes, muesli, raisins, bananas, sweet corn, parsnips, crisps, yam
Moderate GI foods	White and whole meal pasta, oats, barley, porridge, all-bran, grapes, oranges, sweet potato, crisps
Low GI foods	Butter beans, baked beans, chick peas, lentils, kidney beans, apples, cherries, plums, apricots, grapefruit, peaches, milk, yogurt, ice cream

Pre-exercise Nourishment

The limited glycogen stores influence how long you can continue exercising without feeling fatigued. Depleted muscle glycogen causes athletes to "hit the wall" and depleted liver glycogen causes them to bonk or crash. Liver glycogen is fed into the bloodstream to maintain a normal blood sugar level essential for good brain function. Food must be consumed before strenuous exercise to supply sugar to the blood. Athletes with low blood sugar tend to perform poorly because the poorly fuelled brain limits muscular function and mental drive.

This is of particular interest to martial artists because a typical training session will include long periods of physical exercise during which techniques are practiced, then intermixed with technical explanations to help develop technique. If your energy levels are getting low then you will not be fully capable of understanding and learning new technique.

PRE-EXERCISE NOURISHMENT TIPS	
Eat high carbohydrate meals	Snacks eaten within an hour before exercise primarily keep you from feeling hungry and maintain your blood sugar level. They don't significantly replenish muscle glycogen stores. The best refueling occurs within an hour post-exercise.
Exercising for more than 60-90 minutes?	Choose carbohydrates with a moderate to low GI. When eaten an hour before exercise, the foods will be digested enough to be burned for fuel and will then continue to provide sustained energy during the long workout.
Exercising for less than an hour?	Simply snack on any tried and tested foods that digest easily and settle comfortably.
Limit high fat proteins	Fat takes longer to empty from the stomach. Although some athletes find that a small amount of low fat protein will prevent them from feeling hungry.
Be cautious with sugary/ high GI foods	Some people perform well after a pre-exercise sugar fix, but others find that the blood sugar level plummets leaving them feeling tired, light headed and fatigued. If you do eat something sweet, then it is best to eat it 5-10 minutes before exercising. This time span is too brief for the body to secrete excess insulin that causes low blood sugar levels.
Allow time for digestion before exercising	If you have a large meal, wait 3-4 hours before exercising to allow sufficient time for digestion, 2-3 hours for a light meal and about an hour for a small snack.

Reducing Body Fat

For martial artists aiming to lose weight to meet a weight category, it is important that this does not reduce muscle mass as this will result in a loss of performance. The weight loss needs to be targeted as loss of body fat. For many sports people, a weight loss isn't the objective at all. If fat is replaced by muscle then a gain in weight is no problem at all.

The body is composed of two key elements: lean tissue (muscles, organs, bones and blood) and adipose tissue (fat). It is believed that the distribution of fat is more important than the total amount. Fat stored around the abdomen (central obesity) carries a greater health risk than fat stored mainly around the hips and thighs (peripheral obesity).

Men have higher levels of testosterone, which favors deposition around the abdomen, shoulder blades and intestinal organs. Women have higher levels of estrogen, which favors deposition around the hips, thighs, breasts and triceps. After menopause, estrogen levels fall and fat is often transferred to the abdomen from the hips and thighs. Fat stored around the abdomen and close to the intestinal organs can increase the onset of metabolic disorders, high blood pressure, heart disease, maturity onset diabetes (type II) and gall bladder disease.

Fat provides essential fatty acids, absorbs fat-soluble vitamins (A, D and E), is needed for hormone production, provides insulation, gives smooth skin and forms a store of energy. Sources include butter, margarine, and oils. The recommended daily allowance of fat is 10% of the total calorie allowance. Lack of fat in the diet leads to fatigue, inability to absorb fat-soluble vitamins, poor control of inflammation and blood clotting. An excessive intake of fat can lead to obesity, heart disease and certain types of cancer. Any fat that is eaten in excess of body requirements is laid down as adipose tissue. To lose fat you have to eat less while maintaining the same exercise routine. There are number of ways to ensure healthy weight (fat) loss:

KEY POINTS FOR REDUCING BODY FAT	
Lose weight slowly	At a rate of 0.5 to 1 kg per week. If you lose weight any faster, then there is a high chance that it will be muscle, glycogen and water. Crash diets result in 3 kg of glycogen and 3 kg of water loss of the first few days. Don't cut calories too much as it will cause your resting metabolic rate to decrease often by 30-45%, meaning you will need less calories to maintain your weight. The best strategy is to reduce your calorie intake by 500 kcal per day and either maintain or increase you general activity level. Remember that fat loss is not always accompanied by weight loss.
Reduce your fat intake	Aim to consume about 10% of your calories from fat and no more. Excess fat can be laid down rapidly as adipose tissue.
Eat enough carbohydrate	If you eat too little you will experience fatigue and a decrease in training performance. Low carbohydrate diets can result in muscle loss. Choose high fiber filling foods as these will fill you up and satisfy your hunger.
Eat little and often	Aim to eat 5-6 small meals or snacks a day at regular intervals. This will maintain energy levels and prevent hunger and fat storage.
Reduce alcohol intake to aid fat loss	Alcohol is too toxic to be stored in the body and so it is all used up in energy production, preventing the oxidation of fat.
Exercise	This has an after burn effect as adrenaline release causes a higher rate of metabolism to be maintained for 1-2 hours after exercise.
Can't lose weight?	This could be due to underestimating your food intake or yo-yo dieting on a daily or weekly basis. In this case, a diet diary can be useful to keep exact records of food consumption.

Protein

Protein is needed for growth and the formation of new tissues and it can also provide energy. Proteins are made up of amino acids and sources include, meat, fish, pulses, nuts, and dairy. Lack of protein can lead to lean tissue breakdown and a decrease in blood cell replacement. Excess protein is not converted to muscle but to fat, and it can lead to kidney stones, osteoporosis, and colon cancer.

Meats, fish and dairy contain essential amino acids, which cannot be obtained from plant protein sources. The biological value of foods is a measure of how close the match of amino acids is with the body's requirements. Foods with a high biological value include meat, fish, poultry, dairy, and eggs. Low biological value foods include pulses, beans, cereals, and grains.

Meat, poultry, all fish, eggs, beans, nuts, and pulses are important elements of a healthy diet as they contain protein, vitamins and minerals. Meat provides iron, zinc, magnesium, and vitamin B12. Fish oil contains essential polyunsaturated fatty acids that have an important function in reducing the risk of heart disease. Eat two portions of fish each week. Meats on the other hand contain saturated fats that can cause heart disease. Eat these types of foods in moderation.

Calcium, a vital mineral for healthy bones, protein and important vitamins such as A, B12, D, and Riboflavin, is found in milk and dairy products. Try lower fat options such as skimmed and semi-skimmed milk, low fat yogurts, and reduced-fat cheeses. Eat these types of foods in moderation.

How the Body Uses Food

Carbohydrates, protein, alcohol and fat can be used to provide energy (vitamin B and Chromium are also required for the appropriate reactions to take place). The amount and proportion of each fuel used depends on the type, duration and intensity of exercise. For aerobic exercise all 3 fuels may be broken down (protein makes a smaller contribution than carbohydrate and fat). For anaerobic exercise, the main fuel is glycogen and not fat. The amount of carbohydrate (glycogen) used increases with exercise intensity and decreases with exercise duration.

HOW THE BODY USES CARBOHYDRATE, PROTEIN, ALCOHOL AND FAT		
Carbohydrate	4 kcal/g	Carbohydrates are converted to glycogen that is stored in the liver (where it is used to maintain blood sugar level) and in the muscles. There is 3 times as much glycogen in the muscles as the liver. Increasing muscle in the body increases its capacity to store glycogen.
Protein	4 kcal/g	Protein is used by the body for producing energy during intense bouts or prolonged exercise, when glycogen levels have been depleted, for example, marathons. Muscle protein is converted to amino acids that are sent to the liver and converted and stored as glucose/glycogen. This is dependent on exercise intensity, duration, fitness level and pre-exercise diet.
Alcohol	7 kcal/g	Alcohol is absorbed directly in to the blood.
Fat	9 kcal/g	Fat is converted to fatty acids for energy production. Fat burning produces 5 times more energy than carbohydrate burning.

The main cause of fatigue during aerobic exercise is usually glycogen depletion and/or dehydration. The main cause of fatigue during anaerobic exercise is phosphate depletion and/or lactic acid build up, but after several bouts fatigue is usually due to glycogen depletion. The first 90 seconds or so of exercise is predominantly anaerobic, for example weights and sprints. Energy is released, using up glycogen (in the form of glucose) and lactic acid is produced. It is the lactic acid that causes the fatigue and burning sensation. Initially, the balance is about 60% anaerobic and 40% aerobic.

Aerobic energy production levels increase with exercise duration. There are 2 competing reactions that occur in aerobic energy production: carbohydrate consumption and fat consumption. Carbohydrate in the form of muscle glycogen is first used and then glucose from the blood is used (after about 1 hour of exercise). Fat burning becomes dominant after 2 hours of exercise.

Weight Gain Program

Some martial artists may wish to increase muscle mass for personal development. For safe weight making, it is important to control body weight off-season, set realistic targets, and lose/gain weight gradually. There are two requirements to achieve this:

1. Resistance training to provide the stimulus for muscle growth
2. Diet to provide the correct levels of energy and nutrition

How easy this is for an individual is dependent on:
- Genetics: the balance of fast and slow twitch fibers. (Fast twitch fibers generate more power and grow easily.)
- Body type, for example, mesomorph, endomorph, or ectomorph. Mesomorphs tend to increase muscle fast. Ectomorphs increase muscle slower. Endomorphs increase both muscle and fat fast.
- Hormonal balance, for example, testosterone increases muscle growth ability.

Key points about your diet during a weight gain program
- Need to increase calorie intake by around 300-500 kCal
- A good objective is 1-2 lb muscle gain per month
- Eat enough carbohydrate to fuel the body but not so much that you lay down fat
- Remember low GI foods keep glycogen levels up
- Pre-workout carbohydrate should be avoided if trying to lose fat
- Vitamin and mineral requirements will increase during a weight gain program
- Keep well hydrated

Benefits of resistance training
- Helps avoid muscle loss
- Lowers body fat content
- Increases bone mineral density
- Lowers back pain
- Increases metabolic rate
- Increases muscle
- Increases glucose metabolism

Fluids

WATER

Water is the most important nutrient the body needs. The body loses water through the skin, lungs, and gut and via the kidneys as urine, ensuring that toxic substances are eliminated from the body. We also make water when glucose is used for energy production. Water aids the digestion of food, regulates body temperature, lubricates moving parts, and helps transport glucose, oxygen, and fats around the body. As well as drinking water, it can be obtained in the diet from fruits and vegetables. Your individual water requirement will also depend on your activity level and the environment. As the intensity of dehydration increases, it has the following effects on the body:

- Strain on cardiovascular system
- Weight loss
- Dizziness, labored breathing, confusion
- Blood volume decreases and temperature increases
- Nausea, vomiting, diarrhea

ALCOHOL

This should always be taken in moderation. The symptoms of excess alcohol intake are dehydration and intoxication. Once the liver's ability to detoxify alcohol is exceeded the body produces a toxic substance and it is this that brings about headaches. Alcohol decreases coordination, strength, speed, and temperature regulation.

CAFFEINE

Coffee, tea and cola all contain a stimulant called caffeine. If you drink 1-2 cups of caffeine containing drinks a day, it is unlikely to harm your health. Excessive caffeine can lead to nervous, irritable behavior, dehydration, and it affects iron absorption.

SPORTS DRINKS

It is a good idea to hydrate before beginning any exercise and then to rehydrate every 15 minutes after the first 30 minutes of exercise. Sports drinks are to be used before, during and after sport.

VITAMINS AND MINERALS

Although needed in much smaller amounts than fat, protein, and carbohydrate, vitamins are no less important. They activate enzymes in the body that enable many chemical reactions to take place. They are needed to balance hormones, produce energy, boost the immune system, make healthy skin, and protect the arteries. They are also vital for brain and nervous system function. Eating a varied diet will ensure that the body receives all of the vitamins and minerals that it needs. Alcohol, smoking, cooking, and birth control pills all adversely affect the absorption of vitamins and minerals. Like vitamins, minerals are essential for just about every process in the body.

A SUMMARY OF THE USES OF SPORTS DRINKS

		Description	Example	Exercise type
Fluid replacement drinks	Hypotonic	• more diluted than body fluids and contains low amounts of sugars and electrolytes	• < 4 g sugar/100ml • Water • Diet drinks • Low calorie drinks	• < 30 minutes exercise use water • < 1 hour exercise use water/hypotonic drink
Energy drinks	Isotonic	• Contains the same concentration of sugars and electrolytes as body fluids and is absorbed in the small intestine faster than water	• < 4-8 g sugar/100ml • Diluted fruit juices	• 1-2 hours exercise
	Hypertonic	• Drinks with more than 8% carbohydrate • Dehydrating but good for refueling	• > 8 g sugar/100ml fruit juices • fizzy drinks	• 1-2 hours exercise
	Glucose polymer	• Since most people prefer to exercise without food in their stomachs, carbohydrates in the form of glucose polymer drinks can be used • Glucose reaches the blood stream in 15-45 minutes	• 10-20 g glucose polymer/100ml	• > 120 minutes strenuous exercise • e.g. channel swimming

SOURCES AND FUNCTIONS OF VITAMINS

		Source	Function
VITAMINS	A	• Retinol form found in meat, eggs, fish and dairy produce • b-carotene form found in red, yellow and orange fruits and vegetables	Fat soluble, good for vision, antioxidant (slows down the ageing process and protects the body from cancer and heart disease)
	B	Fresh fruit and vegetables	Turns food into energy
	C		Aids immune system, antioxidant
	D	Milk, eggs, fish, and meat. It can also be made in the skin in the presence of sunshine.	Controls calcium balance
	E	Seeds, nuts, and their oils	Protects essential fats from going rancid, antioxidant
MINERALS	Calcium	Vegetables and root vegetables (Calcium alone is found in abundance in dairy produce)	Make up bones and teeth, part of nerve signals vital for brain and muscle function
	Magnesium		
	Sodium	Fruit and vegetables	Make up bones and teeth
	Potassium		Make up bones and teeth, nerve signals vital for brain and muscle function
	Iron	Seeds, nuts, lentils, dried beans, broccoli, whole grains	Oxygen is carried in the blood by an iron compound
	Chromium		Helps to control blood sugar levels
	Zinc		Vital for body repair and development, boost immune system, antioxidant
	Selenium	Abundant in nuts, seafood, seeds (especially sesame seeds)	Boost immune system, antioxidant

Glossary

Blending	—	A movement that negates an attack by "flowing" with an opponent's movements.
Block	—	A defense that gets in the way of a strike. In a grappling context, it is a leg movement that gets in the way of an opponent's legs, potentially tripping them.
Break fall	—	A method of reducing the impact of a fall.
Grappling	—	A way of fighting using grips, hold and locks rather than strikes.
Hold	—	A grappling technique that controls or restricts an opponent's movement
ITF	—	International Taekwondo Federation
Kata	—	A Japanese term that means a prearranged set of movements.
Lock	—	A grappling technique that forces a joint against or beyond its normal range of motion
MMA	—	Mixed martial arts
Pankration	—	Literally means "all powers", reflecting the fact that competitors could use almost any attack that they wanted
Parry	—	A defense that deflects an incoming attack
Randori	—	A way of sparring often translated as "free practice".
Strike	—	An attack that causes damage by impact, for example a punch or a kick.
Takedown	—	A technique that trips, throws or drags an opponent to the ground.
TKO	—	Technical knockout
UFC	—	Ultimate Fighting Championship, US based MMA promotion.
Vale tudo	—	Literally translated from Portuguese this means "anything goes" and refers to the sub-culture of fights in Brazil in the 20th century.
WTF	—	World Taekwondo Federation

Bibliography

Alexander, David, *Aikido and Competition*, www.dragon-tsunami.org/Dtimes/Pages/articlei.htm.

Bean, Anita, *Sports Nutrition (Complete Guide to)*, A & C Black, 2000

Bucksam Kong, Eugene H. Ho, *Hung Gar Kung-Fu*, Black Belt Communications, 1973.

Butcher, Alex, *Judo The Essential Guide to Mastering the Art*, New Holland Publishers, 2008.

Cosser, Sandy, *Can Tainted Taekwondo Overcome Its Sordid Past?*, http://ezinearticles.com

Haines, Bruce A., *Karate's History and Traditions*, Tuttle Publishing, 1995.

Harnsey, Kevin, *Taekwondo*, Connections Book Publishing, 2002.

Hart, Christopher S., *A History of Intercollegiate Boxing*, www.studentorg.umd.edu, 2005.

Hackerott, Tony, *Modern Olympic Taekwondo*, http://ezinearticles.com

International Federation of Associated Wrestling Styles, *International Wrestling Rules*, 2006

Joy, C. Peter, *The Strange and Terrible History of Varsity Boxing*, http://cuabc.org/.,

Kano, Jigaro, *Kodokan Judo*, Kodansha International, 1994.

Karter, Karon and Mezger, Guy, *The Complete Idiot's Guide to Kickboxing*, Alpha Books, 2000.

Kimura, Masahiko, *My Judo*, translation at www.judoinfo.com/kimura2.htm, 1985.

Lindholm, David and Svärd, Peter, *Knightly Arts of Combat - Sigmund Ringeck's Sword and Buckler Fighting, Wrestling, and Fighting in Armor*, Paladin Press, 2006.

Martin, Ashley P., *The Shotokan Karate Bible - Beginner to Black Belt*, A & C Black, 2007.

Martin, Ashley P., *The Advanced Shotokan Karate Bible - Black Belt and Beyond*, A & C Black, 2008.

Martin, N. A., *Yoga for Flexibility, Balance and Strength*, Crowood Press, 2009.

Norris, C. M., *The Complete Guide to Stretching*, A & C Black, 1999.

Ohlenkamp, Neil, *Black Belt Judo Skills and Techniques*, New Holland Publishers, 2006.

Serge, Mol, *Classical Fighting Arts of Japan: A Complete Guide to Koryu Jujutsu*, Kodansha International, 2001.

Sieh, Ron, *Martial Arts for Beginner*, Writers and Readers Publishing, 1995.

Twigger, Robert, *Angry White Pyjamas*, Harper Paperbacks, 1997.

Walter, Donald F., *Mixed Martial Arts: Ultimate Sport, or Ultimately Illegal?*, www.grapplearts.com/Mixed-Martial-Arts-1.htm, 2003.